Understanding Business

Understanding Business

The connections between common sense and good commercial decisions

PHIL DOWELL

C

CENTURY
BUSINESS

First published in 1998 by Century Ltd
Random House, 20 Vauxhall Bridge Road,
London SW1V 2SA

Random House Australia (Pty) Limited
20 Alfred Street, Milsons Point, Sydney,
New South Wales 2061, Australia

Random House New Zealand Limited
18 Poland Road, Glenfield,
Auckland 10, New Zealand

Random House South Africa (Pty) Limited
Endulini, 5a Jubilee Road, Parktown 2193, South Africa

Random House UK Limited Reg. No. 954009

A CIP catalogue record for this book is available from the British Library

Papers used by Random House UK Limited are natural,
recyclable products made from wood grown in sustainable forests.
The manufacturing processes conform to the environmental
regulations of the country of origin.

ISBN 0 7126 7899 9

Typeset by MATS, Southend-on-Sea, Essex
Printed and bound in Great Britain by
Mackays of Chatham PLC, Chatham, Kent

Contents

Section 5 Intelligence at work

SECTION 1

Talking to customers

1. The nature of business

To explore the nature of business, I would prefer us to be able to enjoy a dialogue, but that is not the nature of books. Most of what follows is based on dialogues I have had with people who have themselves been exploring the world of business, starting from all sorts of different places and points of view. In this first chapter of the first section – called 'Talking to Customers' – it seems appropriate for both of us to define our terms of reference.

It is the underlying principle of this book that if the people who work in a business – who are ostensibly there to operate the business – develop a better understanding of *what is happening in the business*, they will find it easier to make sensible decisions. This should – although the process will remain complex – make it much easier for them to work together, and so get on with each other. Some people find this claim quite radical; in my view, it is like saying that the best racing drivers are those who understand their cars. It is common sense.

Work done in the name of business occupies billions of people around the world every day. Most of the businesses place great store on trying to be different from their competitors, so the whole subject area in all its variety is understandably complicated. However, in the final analysis, the same essential activities are to be found over and over again. This book explains what is involved in these essential activities.

What is business?

As you read on, remember this: *a business must sell things, repeatedly, over time, for more money than it spends in so doing.* Otherwise, it ceases to be a business. There are no exceptions.

Let's examine the wording of that statement systematically:

A business — well, the definition of *a business* for the purposes of this book is 'an entity which sells things, repeatedly, over time, for more money than it spends in so doing'. The process of doing this could be called *business*.

must — an imperative, common to all businesses, however special. Any discussion of business which denies the imperative is false.

sell — this does not necessarily imply that representatives of the business need to go forth and persuade or cajole other people to pay for its output. It *does* mean that somewhere there needs to be a person or persons willing to enter into binding agreements to pay money to the business in return for something. These people (often called *customers*) may actually be so keen that they form queues.

The important word is *people*. A computer may place the order, a robot fill it, and a pipe deliver it, but still the ultimate decision – the decision to purchase – involves people. This is vitally important, because people's decisions are influenced by emotional as well as rational factors.

things — it is easier to write 'things' than 'goods, products, or services'. Both tangible and intangible, physical and spiritual, visible and invisible things can be sold. As we will see, it matters less what these things actually are than what the customers perceive them to do. Note that the business does not necessarily have to make or deliver the things, only sell them.

repeatedly — transactions must keep happening. A government may sell its nationalised industries, and a confidence trickster the Eiffel Tower, but these are not the actions of a business. The requirement for transactions to be repeated introduces the first distinction between types of businesses, according to whether the transactions are repeated with the same customers or not.

If not then it may resemble the concept of the 'firm' in basic economics, offering goods for sale in a 'market' to the highest bidder. Some farmers operate like this, literally sending things to auction. It is plausible for the same buyer regularly to be the highest bidder for one farmer's 'things', but presumably neither party would display sufficient trust in the other's commitment – or the fairness of the price, perhaps – to get together and cut out the go-between.

The opposite applies when transactions are repeated with the same customer. Generally speaking – you will come across this phrase often, because there are almost always exceptions to be found as businesses seek to compete at the margins – the buyer and seller in this situation come to know and trust each other, and they form a trading relationship, an essential part of which must be the recognition of a fair price to both parties. Businesses in this category bear little resemblance to the 'firm' in microeconomics, and much of this book is concerned with the reasons why.

over time This is not a repetition of 'repeatedly', but a reference to some concept of permanence. Indeed, survival well may be the primary objective of most businesses. However, 'over time' in the definition is intended also to modify the clause which follows. The business may not instantly sell 'for more money . . .', but it must do so eventually. How soon this 'eventually' comes is an important consideration in the launch of a new business, but the same question applies to established firms. An airline cannot usually pay 'cash' for a new fleet, for example.

for more money this is part definition (money) and part imperative (more). A wealthy philanthropist – or a charity – may wish to sell things for less money than is spent in so doing. The former could be using the price mechanism to ensure that things are receiving commercial distribution; charities sometimes sell things without reference to their true costs, because it makes it easier to persuade people to part with their money this way. Neither example, however, would be called a business.

Everything that happens in business has some monetary consequence, although this is by no means obvious to the vast majority of the millions of people who work in businesses. There are any number of books about organisations, people at work, and management, which seldom mention the word money. They may be interesting and useful, but they are not about business.

The importance of recognising that people's decisions are determined emotionally as well as rationally has already been stressed. Adding money to the equation usually stimulates the former in a big way. Relationships can change dramatically when money becomes involved (think of attitudes to lottery winners, acrimonious divorces, jealousy over someone else's salary) and this goes a long way to explaining why business is a good deal more complicated to be in than it is, for example, to read about.

than it spends in so doing

this means that it is not just the costs of the things that the business sells that have to be counted, but all the other expenses in getting into position to sell those things. This is important, because it is easy to spot the differential between the price of something in a shop, and how much it can be obtained for elsewhere. (The difference can appear staggering, as can be seen on visits to low cost countries. Portuguese ceramics and Indian textiles are good examples.)

The problem is with the *costs of selling* the

things. In the case of a shop, a fixed amount must be spent each week to keep it open, and if it fails to attract enough customers, that is tough. A shop cannot attract customers first, that is, before it even opens. A mail order advertising campaign can do so (although publishers like to know that the things being offered for sale actually exist), but this too involves committing expenditure ahead of customer response.

Uncertainty of this nature is another factor which adds to the complexity of decision-making in business. Where a transaction is being repeated for the umpteenth time, its dimensions will be much more predictable than a completely new proposition. This is one reason why supplier-customer relationships are so difficult to break; they are predictable. Most of the things in your local supermarket have been bought, repeatedly, over time, from the same supplier. The predictability of selling them to the public is a great comfort to both parties. Nevertheless, it remains true that most of the amount you pay for most of the things you buy goes towards the costs of selling – that is to say, the costs of *making the goods available*, rather than the costs of making them.

In fact, the definition we started with does not mention the word 'cost', it says 'spend'. It can be a matter of some argument as to what things actually cost (to be discussed later in the book) for it is essential to understand and allow for the basis on which a 'cost' has been calculated. The chances are, the number quoted as the 'cost' of something has been derived from at least one division sum, and it is necessary to know what assumptions led to the calculation.

There can be no doubting what is *spent* by the business, and it is the inability to pay for something essential – rent, or wages, for

> example – which brings about its demise. It is common for expenditure to precede revenues, and part of managing a business involves arranging to borrow money to ensure that spending is not interrupted. However, *over time*, receipts have to exceed expenditure.

Probably, nothing in the above has surprised you. My guess is that at least once you have said to yourself words to the effect of, 'Of course, but I had not thought of it quite like that.' The next thought may well be, 'If it is so simple, why is the world of work so complicated?' There are two reasons. First, the physical world is complicated; selling newspapers on a street corner is very simple compared to all the activities needed to produce those newspapers, but the latter may not look so complicated compared to the process of prospecting for oil, extracting, shipping, refining it and selling it as petroleum.

As for the second reason why it is complicated, that is because there are people involved. Self-employed people are legally inseparable from the businesses they run, but the vast majority of business activity is undertaken by limited companies. Companies are legal persons (in a specialised sense of the word person), but they are not people; they do however belong to people, employ people, and sell to people. No business exists entirely in its own right; it is the actions and expectations of these three groups of people that form the requirement for the business to 'sell things, repeatedly, over time, for more money than it spends in so doing'.

To fulfil this imperative, the first essential is *talking to customers*. This can be done using advertising, through activities known as marketing campaigns, and via the process of selling. These are the topics of the other three chapters of this section. The next step for the people running a business is *turning activity into money*. From the customer's perspective, things need to be priced. For the business, operations have to be established, service processes designed, and costs calculated. These are the four topics of Section 2. Section 3 is about *facing the wider environment*, and looks at business from the external perspective of consumers, the competitive and cooperative questions raised by the marketing mix, and the essence of business strategy for an established firm, and for its vulnerable predecessor, the new venture. The next section is concerned with *the financial implications of trading*, the familiar subjects of assets and depreciation, working capital, and the use of borrowed money. These topics are often addressed in books which do not mention the word customer; they should not be, for without customers they would not exist. The successful interface between customers and finance results in something called profit. Finally, *intelligence at work* talks about gathering, using, and acquiring it, in alternative senses of the word. Forecasting is speculative, but it produces wisdom; it is assisted by research, and when information is used wisely, it is called – and uses – intelligence. This all adds up to accountability in business.

To make the topics as flexible (and digestible) as possible, the book is written so that you may read the chapters in any order you choose. Each one should make good sense. Some will cover novel or hitherto unconsidered topics, whereas others will confirm ideas that were already suspected or known, but which nevertheless benefit from clarification. You may choose to ignore some topics if they are your specialism, but please do not leave chapters out merely because you think they are unimportant. Each component is an important part of the whole. Think of this book as being in kit form; there are indications of how components interconnect, but it is your job to make the connections. There should not be anything left at the end that you do not recognise.

Everything in business is interconnected, and an ultimate understanding of business means understanding the connections. Unlike the skeleton in the song, it is not a case of 'the leg bone is connected to the knee bone', of one thing just being connected to another in a chain. There are clear relationships between the members of each section, but each chapter (apart from this) has a 'where to next?' paragraph at the end which relates it to a topic in each of the other sections. I can't guarantee there are no closed loops, but I am sure you can look after yourself.

2. Advertising, brands, and consumers

***Selling things repeatedly over time** involves encouraging consumers to form relationships with what they buy. Advertising helps with this, before and after the purchase, but the biggest influence is the brand itself*

Sex will probably get your attention. Well, I can't speak about you personally, but images associated with sexuality will gain more people's attention more easily than most subjects. Advertising sets out to influence people in large numbers. Like the person who claimed that a campaign for British Meat was not effective (because she was a vegetarian), your individual reaction to advertising is not important; what counts is the mass effect.

Because of its undoubted attention-getting ability, the theme of sexuality is used frequently in advertising, to the extent that it sometimes has to be moderated by voluntary codes and indeed, law. Presumably this is why posters advertising power tools found in builders merchants and hire shops feature glamorous women inappropriately dressed to use them (indeed, inappropriately dressed for most things). On the assumption that most people to be found in these outlets are male, the principle must be that the pictures will attract the attention of customers who will then notice the brand name and remember it. This hypothesis can be tested by asking appropriate people to recall the brand name and the posters themselves, although the contribution of the posters cannot be completely isolated in this way. It might happen that some people recall the brand name *Tengo* when it was actually *Squotch* on the poster, in which case the effectiveness of the ploy should be reconsidered. The fact that these posters continue to appear suggests that the recall is broadly accurate however, provided one discounts the alternative – and scurrilous – explanation that the people involved enjoy the making of the posters so much they do not care who remembers them.

Advertising at work

Creating attention and recall is fairly straightforward, but do the images achieve more than that? Are they capable of persuading someone to prefer that particular brand of power tool? The proposition of *identification* – buy this brand and you will resemble the person in the advertisement – can be ruled out in this case, so the supposition is along the lines of 'people who use Squotch tools attract girls like this'. This seems a little fantastic, and the chances are that nobody who actually believed this consciously would be prepared to admit it. As no one believing it subconsciously would realise the fact, it becomes difficult to establish exactly what behavioural mechanism might be enhancing the use of Squotch tools. An approach using the principle of scientific control might be to remove the posters in certain areas with otherwise identical circumstances, and observe any differences in sales patterns. No one really wants to do this though, because their objective is commercial, not scientific, and the amount of money spent on the posters is probably only a relatively small proportion of the total marketing budget.

The juxtaposition of images appealing to the emotions on products from the very practical world of the construction industry is a blunt way of introducing the bilateral domain of purchasing decisions, where both the *rational* and the *emotional* have a part to play. Reading a text like this will put most people into rational mode, so the opening of the chapter is there as a reminder of the other dimension to thought, that of *feelings* as opposed to *facts*. The precise psychological and physiological processes in operation need not concern us here, but given the vast amounts of money spent on advertising and related activities, there is understandably much associated scientific research into generalisable causes and effects. In contrast, the idea that all advertising – or indeed, any advertising – is very cleverly researched and fiendishly constructed by a kind of capitalist thought-police is far-fetched in the extreme. Researching the potential effects of advertisements is very difficult since no one can really say how they will respond until they have seen them (by which time it tends to be too late) and when shown 'story boards' or 'mock ups' what people offer as opinion tends to be firmly based in the rational when it is the emotional response that the advertiser wants to find out about.

There is an added restriction on research, namely that many really different advertising concepts come about when advertisers are changing agencies, and thus do not have the sort of relationship to undertake really extensive – and expensive – research. An agency might undertake research before preparing a new business pitch centring on a new creative theme, but it would be unlikely to risk the sort of expenditure that would be needed to make accurate predictions about the effectiveness of the campaign. As a rule, advertising agencies are quite happy to be responsible for creating awareness, which they seek to measure across the population and over time, for voluntary and prompted recall. They argue, with some justification, that the experience of actual consumption is up to the client to provide.

The scope of advertising

The rational-emotional dimensions, known formally as *cognitive* and *affective*, have similarities with the *left* and *right* sides of the brain. They appear in other forms as well: buying things we are used to, we depend upon *experience* (rational) and also *habit* (emotional); we buy something because *it works*, and also because we *like it*, some things are bought because we *need* them, while for others, it is simply a matter of *want*. In fact, most things that we now need once did not exist, so the idea that the concept of need is entirely based in the rational is incorrect; on the other hand, consuming things we do not need is certainly not rational and must therefore be an emotional phenomenon. The important question for advertising is this: clearly, it can make people aware of things, and it can be shown that this awareness is sometimes strong enough to make some people want to try things, but can it make people *need* things? Can advertising – which people mainly remember for its entertainment value – actually influence people's belief systems to the point that they are persuaded they cannot be without something?

In attempting to do this, it faces a number of dilemmas. In the case of an established product, the issue is, should the advertising be addressed to people who already consume it, or those who don't? Any message that has been a success with the former group can be assumed to have failed with the latter (provided they have been exposed to it), so a change is needed – but what will the effect be of changing the message on those who already buy? Arguing that it will have no effect is to deny the whole purpose of the exercise, so if there is a result, it could well be negative. An ideal answer to the dilemma is to devise different campaigns for different groups of people, but this can only be done provided they can be reached independently and exclusively. 'Girlie' posters for Squotch power tools may be acceptable in a country such as Britain, but they would probably not go down well in Russia where it is common for women to work in construction. Thanks to the regionalised nature of television in the United States, products such as beer can 'align themselves' with major sporting franchises as in 'Bud man, Cub fan' in Chicago, without risking the alienation of fans who do not support the team. In Liverpool or Glasgow, however, there would be severe limitations to a link with one of the local football teams.

Process models

The common model for most consumer advertising – since most advertising is for things which have long since been launched as new – is that of ATR: *Awareness, Trial and Reinforcement.* Advertising can make people aware of brands so that they recognise them when they are shopping, or even go and ask for them. It can make them sufficiently interested to purchase something to find out more about it (the extent to which it can do this will depend on the price of the thing in question) and, after the consumer has consumed whatever is entailed, advertising can add to the experience by enhancing certain aspects of the brand. What it cannot do is make people *like* things, and it is generally acknowledged that most new products do not succeed in achieving lasting consumer acceptance. (To understand something of the challenge presented in creating a new consumer product, try thinking of something you imagine you would really like which is not yet available. It is much easier to think of things than it is to imagine liking them.)

The dilemma for the new product is what to include in the advertisement. There is a theory called the *Elaboration Likelihood Model of Persuasion.* (It may be terminology like this which makes scientific work in consumer behaviour unpopular in the marketing industry.) In this context, *elaboration* refers specifically to the connection between a stimulus such as an aspect of an advertisement, and the person's own related knowledge or experience. A lay, or intuitive, version of the theory is that the greater the elaboration, the more likely the person will be to make a resulting purchase. The ideal then is for the message to contain just the information the reader or viewer needs, and this is roughly what happens with classified advertising which people peruse with a specific purpose in mind. General advertising for something completely new cannot stimulate any elaboration with factual information (for it is something about which the observer has no knowledge), so it has to rely on emotional cues such as an endorsement by a celebrity, or indeed, something emotive and attention-getting like sex appeal. This is only the beginning, though, for once the observer is interested, the advert must then switch to rational mode to explain the benefits of the product. This is frequently too complicated a task to be achieved in one go, as putting too much information into an advertisement dramatically increases the extent of elaboration needed to make someone pay detailed attention to it.

After repeated exposures, a viewer might get more interested in the material content of the total message, but then the emotive part starts to obtrude rather than entertain. (You may have noticed yourself getting a little annoyed by advertisements which you initially found entertaining.) One solution to this problem is to devise a series of messages of increasing complexity: this is achievable in print through special interest magazines where many readers are known to view every issue – and may well be predisposed to elaborate if what you are selling belongs to an area of their enthusiasms, such as an entirely new skin moisturising treatment in a beauty journal or new type of golf ball in a golf magazine. It is harder to deliver on television because the audience is less specialised or consistent. In mass terms, it can be achieved more easily during most popular programmes, but then it is expensive, which is why sequential campaigns tend to be given to best-selling, established products with least associated risk.

There is another model of advertising known as AIDA, which describes a process by which it might influence its audience. Theoretically, an advert should first get *Attention* in whatever way, probably through a totally affective or emotional cue. Then it moves on to develop *Interest* – creating elaboration on factual input. (It does this by expressing the product's benefits, not its features; nevertheless, it is an essentially rational process.) The explanations having been given, the next phase is emotional, for the viewer is expected to develop *Desire* (an important phase, because it is possible to be interested in something without wanting it) after which it is a relatively simple – and rational – *Action* to pick up the phone and place an order, or add the item to a shopping list. Given that the most common reactions to a commercial break on TV are to get up and leave the room, or to flick to other channels, it is not surprising that no one really believes the AIDA model for creative consumer campaigns. Still, it remains a useful *aide-mémoire* for the face-to-face selling process, and it can act as a checklist for copywriting adverts where the reader is already prepared to elaborate, such as for employment opportunities: 'Remember to start with a headline which will *make sure people look. Interest* them in who you are. Make them *want* to join. Tell them *how to go about* applying.' There is one type of TV commercial where this can be seen: in the direct sale of compilation music albums, with invocations to 'bring back the 1970s' and of course, the information that 'this offer is not available in the shops'. If this is the exception that proves the rule, it is because the consumption of music is a wholly emotional subject in which the rational is not an issue. In this instance, the medium really is the message. As a mnemonic, AIDA rolls off the tongue, and has ethereal connotations thanks to Verdi's opera; it is a fair reflection on reality that the prosaic ATR is a more suitable model.

Buying decisions and brands

Purchasing decisions by consumers are set in a three-dimensional world not only spatially, but also according to the extent that the purchase is trivial or important, free or constrained, and frequent or infrequent. Most things sold in supermarkets are bought fairly frequently and are fairly trivial (in the sense of a mistake not being serious). The extent to which they are constrained will be a matter of individual circumstances. An entirely 'free' purchase is, say, a packet of sweets from the checkout display, whereas a totally constrained one might be a specific errand performed on someone else's behalf. Somewhere between, advertisers compete (along with supermarkets themselves) for the roving attention from the shopper which will result in a trial, while competitor products are reinforcing their rational and emotional claims on the shopper's actions. Normally, the latter win, but every so often, people yield to *impulse*, and sometimes, as a rational counterpart, they decide to *experiment*.

Where products are frequently purchased, consumers have tremendous experience upon which to base their decisions, and it is not surprising that brands which are perceived as superior can also usually be measured as superior too by some physical attribute. Nevertheless, feelings have an important part to play in the development and survival of consumer products. At a basic level, a brand is simply a mark which identifies something (as in the branding of cattle), but it has the capacity to carry considerably more information than would otherwise be conveyed by one or two words of language. It is thus a form of shorthand, and with it is commonly associated a guarantee of consistency. (This is not necessarily the same thing as quality; some brands are a guarantee of poor quality, depending on the attributes used for measurement.)

It is not difficult to recognise how abstracts such as trust and attitude come into the perception of brands. The actual experience of consumption remains important, but included with it can be facts – supplied by advertising – of which the buyer might not otherwise be aware, that enhance the value of the purchase in some way. Facts can also be added to the packaging, though once they have been read a few times their message is redundant, so packs which are suitable for message-carrying are reserved for other activities, as exemplified by breakfast cereal promotions. People develop sets of beliefs about products which are 'compiled' into *attitudes*. A brand then becomes more than its physical content: I eat Muncho cereal because I am hungry; I like it as well; I also know that it is good for me because it contains vitamin E and traces of boron. (In truth I am not really sure what boron is, but I am sure they would not bother to mention it on the packet if it were not good for me.) Taken one stage further, I start to believe things about myself that are probably true *because* I choose that brand. Men who eat Muncho cereal are a cut apart, dynamic, thrusting, and in their own sphere of activity, capable of performing with the same panache as Alan Shearer scores goals for England.

Nobody much sees what people eat for breakfast, so the scope is a little limited in this case, but it is only too obvious an influence in people's choice of clothes and accessories. To the purely rational mind, this is completely absurd – but there is no such thing as the purely rational mind, and it is not absurd. As we watch the teenagers who will lead us through the twenty-first century walking around in a Tiger Woods hat, wearing a replica Ryan Giggs shirt, and trainers 'just like' Michael Jordan's, or appearing to identify simultaneously with all of the Spice Girls, it is perhaps a perfect expression of the emotional confusion – turmoil even – that being a teenager entails. (It seems that rebellion has always entailed conformity with one's mates.) To those people who insist on denying the role of the emotions in marketing – and thence in business – the question is simple: do you also deny having been a teenager?

Brand personalities

Brands definitely acquire personalities of their own, and serious research is undertaken aimed at encouraging consumers to articulate their feelings about the personalities of products they buy regularly. It is used by brand managers to explore the scope available to them in dealing with the user/non-user dilemma, since new images in promotions ought to be acceptable to existing users if they are consistent with a brand's personality. In the case of so-called 'executive cars', the brand personality is sufficiently powerful that aspiring buyers will not include certain marques on their lists for factual research and test driving unless the personality effect is acceptable. You only have to think about the circumstances in which people – men, mainly – insist upon commuting alone in their cars to realise that there is often an exceedingly complex relationship between a man and his motor.

Where a human personality is actually subservient to – or expressed through, as you prefer – the personalities of the brands the person chooses, this phenomenon is referred to as a projection of situational self-image. This could not arise without publicity, and frequently has something to do with advertising. (Someone once remarked that if you can create a public image without advertising, it is immensely valuable. Unfortunately, it was John Delorean, whose credentials were rather discounted after his eponymous motor car factory closed with losses to creditors and HM Government before any cars were sold.) Awareness is important in ostentatious brands, since it matters to the consumer to be seen, for example, to carry Louis Vuitton luggage or wear a Rolex watch. This depends upon other people recognising the choice, and of course, these have to be 'the right' people. A division develops between mass and exclusive brands in such circumstances – for so-called adults. Exclusivity is essentially at odds with market share, so for frequently purchased goods, exclusive brands tend to be small scale affairs where the commercial objective is to sell out available production capacity for the maximum revenue. The products actually have to be high quality as well.

In the final analysis, persistent advertising claims which are unsupported by the products they represent fail, much as the marketing industry would like to have the final say. The person who wrote the slogan 'great taste, great value' (which appears on a pack, not an advert, in fact) may have been particularly pleased at coming up with something undeniable. It features on packets of catfood, so the human cannot comment on the taste, nor the cat on the value. The cat can refuse to eat it, though, and has the last miaow.

WHERE TO NEXT?

Advertising and branding are important elements in premium pricing (Chapter 5)
They are some of the variables that determine consumer behaviour (Chapter 9)
Successful branding results in superior profits (Chapter 16)
Research helps to direct advertising (Chapter 18)

3. Marketing campaigns – the 6Ms

Selling things repeatedly over time *involves making decisions about what to tell whom, and how to go about it*

The term 'marketing' has many subtleties of meaning, and is used in two different contexts. Sometimes called strategic marketing, it refers to the overall conceptual basis on which business decisions should be taken. One definition for this context is 'that part of the business which is concerned with customers'. According to this book, *every* part of the business is concerned with customers, so perhaps it should be renamed *Understanding Marketing.* As well as being misleading, this would also be unfair; whatever its meaning, 'marketing' does not have exclusive rights to be concerned with customers. Besides, there is another, functional, use of the word, to refer to those activities and people who inform actual and potential customers about the things the business wishes to sell. Their specific activities are known as marketing campaigns, for which there is a useful checklist[1] called The 6Ms.

The six Ms of the marketing campaign derive from the need to communicate with customers, actual or potential. There must be a *message*, therefore, and to carry it, a *medium* is required. The message can be as simple as: 'Eat at Joe's' or it can be quite complex – '(use all your senses to) try this free sample of instant coffee'. The medium used also varies in complexity, from a name-only placard at a sports ground, to a party plan demonstration of waterless cooking. Sometimes the message will determine the medium (and, extrapolating from just the examples so far, they are obviously closely related); however, something else is needed to determine the message, namely the

---

[1] As with all checklists, make sure the context is suitable before using it; there is nothing more depressing than the mindless application of an inappropriate formula.

motive for the campaign. There should be a purpose and expectation behind every campaign, though they may not all produce results. 'We know only half our advertising works – the trouble is, we don't know which half!' is a saying which has been attributed to various famous business people, among them King Gillette (his name, not his title), founder of the razor and toiletries empire. The statement was intended to emphasise the difficulty of isolating the precise effects of advertising, and thus defend the expenditure to critical investors. Too often, it has been proffered subsequently as an excuse for an ill-conceived campaign, as in 'we need only get it right half the time'.[2]

No one should undertake a campaign without knowing what they want people on the receiving end to do in response. It may be a very weak outcome, as in: 'we advertise on the perimeter of televised football matches so that people won't say "Who?" when our reps introduce themselves and their company. There is no point in trying to say more; the simplest message is our name. We use televised football because our target audience is middle-aged males.' This is acceptable, but if you have shares in a company which advertises at sports grounds solely because it is 'good for the corporate image', consider selling them.

It is usually the case that this year's marketing budget is a certain percentage of last year's sales. It should be the other way round – a percentage of next year's sales, which its spending will generate – but it is does not work that way, as trends in advertising expenditure during recessions indicate. Amongst other things, this confirms the difficulty of predicting the outcome of marketing campaigns as expressed by King Gillette. If money could be spent with confidence during downturns, surely it would be.

There may be no absolute standard of what to expect in sales revenue from a pound spent on marketing, but there is still a considerable value in determining the relative effectiveness of the alternatives available. This introduces two more Ms:

---

[2] Actually it was not advertising which really launched King Gillette's empire – the message was too complex – but his personal ability to persuade the US Army authorities that his safety razors were preferable to the traditional cut-throats for soldiers serving in the First World War trenches. Advertising may have followed, to try to convince the soldiers who subsequently returned home to persevere with safeties, possibly against difficult odds, for the technology had a long way to go compared with today's shaving equipment.

measurement and *money*. For some campaigns, measurement will be straightforward, as with returned coupons or phone messages. In other circumstances, it may be necessary to undertake additional, specific activity, such as street or telephone interviews leading to statements like: 'of a sample of middle-aged males asked to name insurance companies, football watchers were 50 per cent more likely to mention Intergalactic Insurance.'

Where a large amount of money is to be spent, a certain amount of measurement needs to be undertaken in advance – testing the clarity of a message, judging its potential to achieve the motive – in order to estimate the effects of the campaign proper. Firstly, this should demonstrate – as far as it is possible to do so – that the money will be well spent. Secondly, it will be necessary in some circumstances – staffing telephones for example – to anticipate the level of response in order to be ready for it.

The word 'money' should perhaps read 'cost effectiveness', but, apart from the fact that 'The 5 Ms and a C' loses something as a checklist title, it is worth remembering that *doing it for money* is implicit in the definition of business. Money sits at the bottom of the list as an apt reminder that marketing is not just a game or a pleasant alternative to work, a fact which the more idiosyncratic members of the marketing industry sometimes appear to forget.[3]

If money is at the bottom of the list, then the sixth M must come at the top, describing the starting point for the process of devising the campaign. 'Marketplace' is an acceptable term to describe the environment in which the business is trading and into which the campaign must penetrate. 'Map' could also be used, implying a description of the territory on which the campaign is to be waged, however, I prefer *matrix*.

Let's begin at the beginning:

The matrix

There are a number of meanings for the word 'matrix' including: 'the space in which anything is formed', and its use in this context is to represent the 'birthplace' of the campaign. The

[3] No doubt they are cultivating an image!

starting point is an analytical phase to reveal the important factors in the matrix, upon which the campaign will be built. You cannot begin with the creative part and find a context to fit it to; as with any construction, it must have a solid foundation. It is for such reasons that marketing has been termed *the scientific art*. There are a great many factors influencing buyer behaviour as well as the campaign being planned, starting with the 'natural inertia' with which people ignore messages.

Matrix also has a familiar mathematical usage, being a rectangular array of variables such as a spreadsheet. There are frequently more than two sets of factors influencing buyer behaviour, but in the two-dimensional case, individual cells are found at the intersection of variables (for example, the people's age and their TV watching habits), which are to be related to buying patterns. The universe – the term used for all potential buyers – can thus be divided up. If the different cells demonstrate different patterns, this starts to suggest a range of different motives that would influence the people represented. If the patterns are not different, then one or more of the variables is irrelevant for this purpose, and may be removed from the analysis. It may be highly significant in other contexts, of course. For example, gender is a big factor in the purchase of toiletries, but not of cigarettes.

If this implies a method of trial and error to find the relevant factors or variables, that is because such an approach is required, although supposition and experience help with the initial guesses. It usually comes as a great disappointment to a few people discovering marketing for the first time that there is no answer to the question, 'OK, what's the formula?' The fact remains that there is no universal template which can be laid over a marketing problem to reveal 'the answer'; you have to treat each case on its merits. You would not expect a biologist to use an identical approach to study whales and termites, or a physicist to study sub-nuclear particles and stars with the same equipment. You should not expect to find many immediate similarities between your mother buying a packet of breakfast cereal, an Air Force chief buying a fighter plane, and yourself buying a pair of shoes.

The effort in matching the influencing factors to the situation can be well worth it. If the different cells that emerge are observed to display pronounced differences in buyer behaviour, these are called *segments*, possibly the single most useful concept in marketing. The existence of segments cannot always be guaranteed, and even if different patterns can be observed amongst buyers, they are only helpful if it is possible to tell in advance who will do what. The value of a segment is that you can send it a message, and have a good idea how its members will respond. Too often, marketing campaigns are sent to *sectors* which are groupings (for instance, manufacturing companies within the M25) not based on buying patterns. This can result in a segmented response – what appeals to some, others may hate – and is not particularly desirable, even if it is seemingly the 'best' that can be done. Do not mix up segments and sectors.

Identifying reliably which variables or factors will be at work in a given situation requires research. It can be useful to speculate about what they might be in advance, because research is usually more efficient if it is testing a hypothesis. It is important *not* to make careless assumptions and confuse factors which are well correlated but have different implications (for instance, children are the main sweet *eaters*, but mothers are the main sweet *buyers*). Research into buying patterns for frequently purchased consumer goods shows that there are so many factors at work as to make the process effectively a matter of probability and statistics. Statistical methods can be used to form clusters of people representing segments, but generally, it is helpful if a human mind can process the variables simultaneously, to the point of 'visualising' typical segment members.

The simplest matrix is two-by-two, and there is a form of preliminary check which should be applied, according to whether the thing being sold is a frequently or infrequently purchased item (for a given individual), and whether the individual is buying for the first time, or repeating a purchase. The actual experience of the purchase and the subsequent use of the thing purchased dominate other factors, but obviously it is not present in a first time purchase. (Think of the mess you have sometimes made buying something for the first time.) An experienced consumer of a frequently purchased item is extremely well informed about that item, and cannot easily be influenced by distantly-related or spurious claims. A repeat purchaser of an infrequent item such as a domestic appliance has only a limited knowledge. It may in fact be biased by past experience, which may be out of date, and inaccurately recalled. Such a person can literally be an awkward customer.

After this stage, there are generally three dimensions to be considered. These are the *characteristics* of the buyers (factors independent of the purchase: such as age, sex, location, home owning for consumers; and industry, size, location, ownership for businesses), and the *circumstances* (what is causing the purchase, such as impulse, habit, crisis, Christmas, getting married, opening a new branch). The third dimension is that of how potential buyers respond to the norms or expectations set by the competitors in the marketplace (if you wish, you can make this word begin with C by calling it *choice*), such as price range, quality, availability, service, alternatives and substitutes. There are many more headings in each category, and by now, it should be obvious why there is no standard 'formula'. The purpose of the exercise is to identify a motive which will influence someone's potential or actual buying behaviour, and this must depend in part on both the person and the thing being sold.

The motive

The process of identifying suitable segments to be attacked is known as *targeting.*[4] If it is possible to target a selected segment (it may not be – there has to be a suitable medium), the *motive* in so doing more or less appears automatically, as a natural consequence of the analysis and decision.

There is an immediate distinction to be made between changing behaviour and reinforcing it. Consumer advertising can do both to some extent, but one of the biggest problems for the marketing departments of fast moving consumer goods companies is how to stimulate new consumers without promotions falling into the hands of existing ones who would have bought the brand anyway at normal prices. Money-off packs, or two-for-the-price-of-one offers on supermarket shelves are most likely to be noticed by people looking for that brand, and least likely to attract people who do not buy that product category. One legitimate and often excellent technique is to promote one thing on the back – sometimes literally (of the packaging) – of another.

In fact there are only a limited number of possible motives, and they can be ranged on a kind of continuum from 'become aware' to 'make a purchase'. The precise nature of the stages

---

[4] Military terms in marketing are unfortunate; remember you are trying to make friends with a target audience, not shoot it.

varies, as ever, according to the context. Here is a sample list for an insurance product:

Create awareness of name
Impart knowledge of company's business
Present a certain image
Overcome misperception
Present product facts
Permit appointment to be made (passive response)
Encourage enquiry for more information
Request quotation
Request appointment (active response)
Send or phone in order

The exact range will obviously be different for different things being sold. For a motor car, it would include:

Introduce a new model
Introduce a local dealer
Ask for a detailed brochure
Request a test drive

The test drive could additionally be done two ways, with and without some kind of incentive.

The hierarchical aspect is important; people will not request a test drive if the marque of a car does not appeal to their self-image, for example. The element of trial is significant, and there is a big distinction to be made between things which someone purchases frequently (which are relatively low value and therefore low risk), and things like cars, which are bought infrequently and are seriously expensive. With the former, the motive is usually to induce a trial, with a coupon to purchase cheaply or free, or a free sample. Sellers of big, infrequent purchases cannot do this, and the process is accordingly more complex for both parties. In all circumstances, the message should make it clear what the recipient is expected to do next. Thus, there can only be one motive per message.

The message

A message delivered person to person can theoretically be

tailored precisely to the customer's circumstances, but only if the latter is prepared to make it a two-way communication. Anyone who has ever worked in sales will tell you that the hardest thing to cope with is the tight-lipped poker-faced character who listens to the presentation and just says 'No' at the end. Marketing messages are essentially one-way, preparing the ground for future dialogues with the more promising prospects.

The biggest issue is that mostly, the message is not welcome, or at least, it is uninvited. It is human nature either to satisfy or sublimate needs, so people are not easily found who are just waiting to hear about exactly what is on offer, having been wondering for some time where to get it. Indeed, when they are, and the message is welcomed, remarkable results can be achieved. The band Take That set statistical records in the early nineties for chart entry because the fans received letters telling them exactly when new singles would be released. As a result over half of them regularly went to the record shops on the same day.

Unfortunately the neutral or unwelcome message first has to get attention before it can impart information. Unsolicited direct mail promotions now arrive containing offers within offers, with prize draws and free gifts and other attractions not remotely connected to the thing actually being marketed. The fact that they continue to come through letter-boxes would suggest that the concept works, despite the apparent high cost involved. It is worth considering that if the thing in question is a magazine, and the promotion results in a subscription by direct debit which lasts five years, the promotional budget can appear to be quite high compared to the initial revenue generated. Still, there is an awkward balance to be struck between impact and import, and TV commercials – fighting against the increasing tendency by viewers to surf on remote control through channels at breaks – are becoming more and more complex, to the extent that it can be necessary to watch several times just to find out what is being advertised. This may get attention, but whether it is good advertising is not clear.

Usually, the marketing plan acknowledges the dilemma by resolving into a two-stage process, being the attention-interest, and the interest-information phases. Certainly, most consumer sales not involving shops first invite the potential customer to display interest (send for a brochure, have a free trial, consent to an interview, etc). Expressions of interest are then followed with information and various attempts at conversion to a sale.

With smaller businesses, the choice of an appropriate message is often a subjective, hopeful act. If it then transmits something of the 'personality' of a business proprietor, this may be quite effective. What is to be avoided is the 'committee' decision which puts the message through a number of modifications based on the subjective preferences of the contributors. When the campaign is significant or expensive, the message – or a range of alternative messages – need to be tested first. This process costs money and slows down the campaign. (It is a funny thing about marketing campaigns that they so often seem to be running late.) The choice of medium will at least limit the range of options for the message.

The medium

The means for carrying a marketing message may well be determined by or implicit in the choice of segment. Middle-aged-male-TV-football-watchers are probably not identifiable by other means, so it follows that pitch perimeter advertising is the choice. Middle-aged-male-fishing-enthusiasts may require a different medium, perhaps a loose insert in an angling magazine. The complexity of the message is also a factor. The camera does not stay on a hoarding long enough for a viewer to take down a phone number, nor can the message be made intriguing enough to invite phone calls. A commercial break at half time would be required to achieve this, with distinctly different cost implications.

Consumer campaigns are usually, though not always, directed at a large audience, but business to business marketing can be quite selective, in which case, the numbers involved also play a significant part in determining the medium. The two phases of 'generating leads' and 'converting prospects' both have implications for the resources needed to handle the response, and therefore the money involved. Whether it is preferable to seek a high initial response level and a low conversion rate or vice versa is one of those issues which can only be resolved by examining the process in its entirety. Sending out large numbers is desirable for those using low cost mail order brochures, but less so for those sending the traditional one-thousand-page catalogues, who therefore use purchase incentives. Salespeople like appointments with high conversion potential. They use the term 'confirmed leads' – the equivalent of 'enquiries' in mail order – to distinguish them from 'cold calls'.

Sometimes the two phases in the process will be seamless, as with telephone sales where the caller first establishes that the listener is relevant and interested before proceeding with the full talk. Other businesses use telephone calls solely to set up appointments for representatives. As the potential audience increases in size, so the medium inevitably becomes less intimate. This gives rise to a sort of hierarchy for the first phase, which, for a targeted manager in a business to business context, might look like this:

Arranged introduction
Personally arranged meeting
Formal invitation (hand-written)
Personal phone call
Assistant to assistant phone call
Genuinely personalised letter
Assistant to contact phone call
Electronically personalised letter
Telesales phone call
Impersonal mail shot
Targeted/specialised advertisement
General advertisement

The sense of hierarchy is straightforward, even if it is possible to argue over the sequence of some of the entries in the list. Should telesales perhaps come before electronically personalised letter? It used to be the case that if you could phone why bother to write first. Write afterwards, when you have a better idea of what to say, having spoken to the target. Latterly, the advent of voice-mail and answering machines means that the telecanvasser's renowned skirmishes with the traditional 'they shall not pass' secretary have now become a case of man or woman against machine. Machine wins hands down, of course. Hence, a letter may have a better chance.

Every category offers detailed sub-choices – the letter, for example, may be sent by telex, fax, e-mail, post or courier – and there has been some time during the last forty years where each of these has been almost certain to get a response. (In 1971, there was an extended postal strike, and hand-delivered letters were such a novelty that they could not fail.) The fax, meanwhile, has lost its sense of urgency and importance in less than fifteen years of existence.

A hierarchy for the second phase medium might be:

Joint working party
On-going negotiations
Lunch (or breakfast!)
Personalised presentation (away from the prospect's office)
Group presentation/reception/seminar
Sales visit
Video
Second phone call
Sample mailing
Catalogue mailing
Brochure and order form

It can very easily become a multi-stage process. The choice of how persistent to be depends upon what proportion of the enquiries being generated have to be converted to sales. This is where the importance of measurement comes in.

Measurement

It seems obvious that the outcome of a campaign should be measured, yet many people forget to do it. Perhaps the excitement and the extra work involved in handling the response causes them to leave it until later. The task then loses its urgency until the next time a campaign is planned when, suddenly, there is not time to go through all the previous responses. Businesses that work this way deserve no sympathy for their inability to spend marketing budgets wisely. The sensible time – and the most efficient – for measuring response is as it happens.

It can be difficult sometimes to measure the effect of an awareness campaign, or to isolate the particular impact of just one of many pieces of activity but, provided the cost is reasonable compared to the overall budget, it is worth doing. An advertising agency should want to measure awareness for the sake of its own achievement, though it may expect the client to pay. Timing is actually critical in this instance with measurements being made during the life of the campaign, and of the subsequent 'decay' after it is over.

There should be little difficulty in measuring the effects of a direct response or telephone campaign, because these activities automatically generate data which can be counted. Part of the process of managing a telesales activity should involve the operatives writing down the numbers called, people spoken to, and outcomes.[5] Incoming phone calls can be logged as they happen by the team fielding the enquiries; sophisticated telephone equipment can record the numbers, though not yet the outcomes, automatically. Returned post cards and coupons should be counted and filed as they are processed.

Businesses have been known to stick hand-written enquiry coupons received to envelopes and mail them back to the people who sent them in, because it is easy. This is a false economy, and a very short-sighted way of handling response. Subject to any legal restrictions, enquiries should be kept on file for use at a later date. Firstly, a follow-up to those not responding in due course may be productive; with the best will in the world, people do not always get round to doing everything they should. Secondly, the names can be used again on a future occasion. They are people who have expressed an interest. If they do not subsequently buy, it is possible that the time was not right, or that something interfered with their intentions, which makes them good prospects for the future. Of course, some could have considered the offer thoroughly, and definitely decided against it. It is important therefore to attempt to examine what has *not happened* from a campaign, as well as what has.

Certainly, the campaign needs to be measured all the way through. It may be that football-watchers' recall of Intergalactic Insurance is higher than the norm, but if it subsequently transpires that only one in twenty takes out a policy (the others spend all their money on satellite TV subscriptions), while one in four anglers are converted, the fishermen may be a better bet. The cost per thousand reached may be higher through the loose insert in the magazine, as may the cost per enquiry received, but what matters is the cost per sale generated; the point of spending marketing money is to get it back.

---

[5] It seems that telesales now do this directly on to computer databases, although it may be illegal if the respondent's permission is not obtained.

Money

The epithet for marketing, 'scientific art', is summed up neatly when money is considered. If the science is to be found in measuring the results, the art is clearly in creating something which is exceptional in performance. The other unanswerable question ('What's the formula?' is the first) is, 'How much should a campaign cost?' – or variations on the same theme of cost-effectiveness. There is too much unpredictability about sending out unilateral messages. A large magazine group happily quotes the unexpected way in which the public responds to its Reader Offers. It is possible to predict with some accuracy what the total response will be after the first few days' orders have come in, but quite impossible to predict the first few days' response itself. Mostly, the magazine earns (by taking a margin on the offer) a contribution roughly equal to the revenue it would receive if it sold the space as advertising, but every so often there is a bumper issue which captures the public's imagination, causes panic in the office, and makes a lot of money.

Where an activity or campaign, or enough common components thereof, are repeated with some regularity, then it starts to be possible to average out the cost per response, and weed out the consistent under-performers. It is much more difficult if each campaign is inconsistent. To decide what is an acceptable average expenditure, efforts can be made to compare with what competitors appear to achieve. (This is easiest to do for advertising, where every exposure is monitored by an independent agency called MEAL and priced according to published rate cards.) Marketing expenditure is then calculated as a percentage of relevant sales for different competitors. This has a certain value, but the comparisons are not so useful if competitors are pursuing distinctly different motives.

The other problem with such comparisons, which is bad news for businesses with small shares of the market, is that there are considerable scale advantages to marketing as the size of campaign increases; media can be bought more cheaply, the fixed costs of the operation (creativity, artwork, typesetting) are spread across a greater volume, and with consumer goods, more of the message falls on receptive ears. In comparison, the low share competitors' own efforts cost more each and are more haphazard in whom they reach.

With business to business marketing, the question of how much to spend is further complicated by the value of the outcome. If it is merely a sale, then a percentage of some sort will apply, but if the campaign results in a successful continuing relationship with new customers, how much is that worth? Somewhere in between is the idea of building a reputation. It is often said by firms who supply occasional purchases that although they cannot directly identify response to individual marketing campaigns, they notice a decline in orders if they discontinue their campaigning.

Where new customers are being recruited, the answer is likely to be that the budget for the campaign should be determined by other factors. Some idea of the desired response (how many enquiries could be safely handled and easily converted), should be 'plugged into' a forecast of the campaign at work. This in turn generates numbers for the size and scope of the campaign, from which quotations for work from relevant suppliers can be turned into a budget. If the budget is deemed to be 'too much' for some external reason, the worst thing that can happen is a compromise on the quality of the material used. To borrow an advertising slogan, you never get a second chance to make a first impression, so what is the likely effect of a poor quality campaign?

Designing the campaign to be delivered in batches, rather than all at once, is another method of compromise which may not prevent some loss if it does not work as expected, but at least means that the losses can be cut at some point. If it is necessary to operate with an absolutely limited budget then it is preferable to identify a single segment in which an effective, quality campaign can be targeted, but it means all-eggs-in-one-basket. The alternative is a weak, broadly-spread attempt which probably goes off like a damp squib in all directions.

WHERE TO NEXT?

Marketing campaigns should reflect the overall quality of the operations they promote (Chapter 6)

They form part of the market mix (Chapter 10)

Stock levels supporting campaigns affect working capital requirements (Chapter 14)

Anticipating the roll-out of the campaign begins the forecasting process (Chapter 17)

4. Selling – a tough proposition

__Selling is a must__, but when customers don't know, or even think, they want to buy, it is also a challenge

In Heinz Goldman's classic book on creative selling, *How To Win Customers*, there is the story of a life insurance salesman who pathetically approaches another man with the words: 'I don't suppose you would like to buy any life insurance?' It happens that the 'prospect' is a sales manager, who decides on the spot to take out a small policy, with the twin objectives of boosting the rep's confidence, and then commenting on his poor style. After the transaction is settled, the sales manager approaches the subject of the other's lack of technique. He is quickly taken aback when the salesman replies, 'Of course I know that is not normally a good approach. I just happened to notice that you were a sales manager, so I gave you my specially reserved pitch. Sales managers are impossible to sell to any other way.'

It is difficult to say whether this actually happened, or whether in the interests of driving home the truth the author made it up.[1] It certainly demonstrates that the selling process can involve the unexpected. The life insurance industry, being thoroughly familiar with the concepts it represents – and the good sense associated with them – struggled for years to come to terms with the fact that talking about what would happen to someone's family if he were knocked over by a bus the following day, while it contained a real, important message, failed to sell any insurance. The problem is that the message is so real as to

---

[1] I could not find this reference in the edition I currently have (earlier ones have been borrowed), so perhaps I imagined it. Alternatively, it may have been edited out of an earlier edition after sales managers threatened to stop recommending the book to their representatives. *How To Win Customers* by Heinz Goldman is published by Pan, in numerous editions.

be threatening; it frightens the prospect, and may also induce guilt feelings about the way he spends his income. The listener's instinct then is to try and escape from the situation – to close the conversation. The industry discovered the solution eventually – let the conversation be about the fate of the prospect's family had he been knocked down *yesterday*. This way, he is reassured (he wasn't knocked down), but the message is still there, and the prospect can almost be grateful to the representative for pointing it out. This approach worked well, though it too was abandoned when reps realised that if they sold policies not as insurance but as savings plans, they fared so much better. Amongst other things, they appealed to greed, rather than prudence, as a motive.

Messages

The above demonstrates how the buying process – whether someone is actively selling or not – involves a mixture of the rational and the emotional. More formally, these dimensions are known as the cognitive and the affective, the former dealing with knowledge, and the latter feelings. Messages such as the impact of tomorrow's bus create what is known as 'cognitive dissonance', meaning that the listener does not like the message, and seeks to ignore it. The reason that different health warnings appear on cigarette packets is that each one is dissonant, but as the smoker gets used to it, so it can be ignored. One message is fairly ineffectual. Varying the messages means that every time smokers see a new one, they have to work harder on the process of ignoring it. Cognitive dissonance is an extreme case of the more general selling problem, namely that it is not always enough for people to *need* something, they must also *want* it. The trouble is, response to dissonant messages cannot be predicted. You might think that news of soldiers getting shot would discourage applications to join the army, but in fact it does the opposite.

Products like life insurance and encyclopaedias, things for which there is a clear need, derived from good intentions, have to be sold actively, because people do not otherwise get round to buying them. Goldman's book is about *creative selling*, meaning the securing of sales which would not otherwise happen. Some people view selling as undesirable and exploitative; the response of people working in sales to such detractors objecting to the 'foot-in-the-door' intrusion is to observe that they are engaged in the effective presentation of ideas of mutual benefit. They then back up the assertion with stories of mutual success. Creative selling is always required, for this reason: until people know what it is someone is selling, and fully appreciate the benefits it offers them, how can they decide whether they need it? All but the most basic needs for food and clothing have been acquired as a result of social development, and were once unknown. To claim that something is not needed as a matter of principle is to deny human progress. The creative sales rep's job is to go forth and point out the need – and then to create the desire to satisfy it. If intrusive approaches are sometimes required, this is merely to get someone's attention. This is a fact, though the jury is probably still out on the extent to which the end justifies the means in every situation.

Needs

Because of the complex interplay between the rational and the emotional, identifying and satisfying needs has to be done on an individual basis. A single message for the population is called an advertisement, and while advertising has a role to play in influencing attitudes, it is pretty ineffective in actually making people decide to buy things. Many products that we take for granted today – meaning that we go to shops and buy them – started life facing big selling hurdles. Vacuum cleaners were sold door to door by highly motivated, 'evangelical' salesforces. The basic proposition is that vacuum cleaners are effective at removing dust, a definite need now, and possibly even more pronounced in the days when vacuums were a novelty and people used coal fires. Surely they would walk their way into people's homes? Well, we do not know how effective by today's standards early vacuum cleaners were, but technical performance is a cognitive issue. Where they failed was not on the effective, but the *affective* front. The proposal that I need a vacuum cleaner – a machine to help me keep my house clean – is a clear suggestion that currently, I am not capable of doing so. Well, I do not wish to be told that. To overcome this negative message, the foot-in-the-door evangelists had to give demonstrations showing how their automated cleaners would *enhance my performance of the task.* The machines were really sold because of their attachments, and not the basic function we know today. (It enables us to live with fitted carpets instead of having to take them up and beat them twice a year.)

An added complication with negative connotations for vacuum cleaners was that they arrived at a time when many of the people most likely to be able to purchase them were just beginning to realise that they could no longer afford domestic servants. Since those days, we have become used to labour saving devices, yet there is one which has yet to become universal in British homes – the dishwasher. Washing machines for clothes were not so difficult to sell when they first appeared, as they replaced the process of heating water in a copper, and the need to agitate the washing by hand – straightforward rather than radical steps. People continued to use mangles to remove water from the clean clothes, either those they already owned, or which came as an integral part of the new machine. The radical step was the introduction of the spin dryer, which initially came alongside the by now familiar washer, in the 'twin tub' format. Though these were always available in shops, their success depended upon another evangelical salesforce. Its members made a fuss of how much cheaper they were (cutting out the middleman) but in reality, it does not matter how cheap something is to someone who does not want it. What the salesforce did was create the need for spin dryers (the contemporary response being, 'I don't need one, I've got a mangle'). Once people were used to spin dryers, the process of converting to a single drum, fully automatic machine which most people now possess and certainly accept as necessary, was straightforward.

Objections

However, this has not yet happened with automatic dishwashers, and this fact means that people are not generally well-informed about them. Here is a list of explanations commonly given by people in discussion groups for not having a dishwasher:

Cannot afford one
They don't work properly
Too expensive to run
Only two people in the house

No space to put it
Not hygienic
Take too long to stack
Don't do saucepans
No crockery to wash
I like washing up

In traditional sales training parlance, these would be called objections. As each is raised, a counter-argument can be given to the rational element. Several of them are misperceptions which can be countered thus: older models did not work so well, but the latest do; they cost less than a washing machine to run; two people can make good use of one, you can 'save up' a load; they wash at a higher temperature than by hand, and dry in hot air, which is more hygienic. Sadly, the effect of this series of factual 'victories' for the sales pitch is not to win people over; instead, they get more and more irrational. Continuing to counter objections, it is true that machines take time to stack, but less than washing up by hand would, and anyway, it's what they *do do* that counts, not what they don't, so never mind saucepans. This 'putting down' only results in what are more or less lies – there may be a few people with no crockery in the house, but is there really anyone who positively enjoys washing up? In a rational world, only two of these objections have any validity, but they all have to be dealt with in the selling process – and in the selling process, winning an argument often means losing a sale.

Implied criticism

There is a fundamental point to understand about the selling process. Selling something to a person who has not previously bought from that sales rep (or a predecessor) will always cause problems. Occasionally, an enquiry is received from someone who has just decided for themselves that they want to buy the very thing on offer (such leads are manna from heaven for salespeople) and even more rarely, a rep encounters someone who is in the very process of deciding.[2] However, it is human

---

[2] An event like this could lead to the following exchange at the rep's office: 'How did you manage to close the sale so quickly?' 'I got lucky: it was just what the customer was looking for.'

nature either to satisfy needs or to sublimate or rationalise them away, and hence the proposition 'buy this' is perceived to imply an element of disapproval. The rep is telling the prospect that the decision not to buy is wrong, either for not wanting (needing) whatever it is, or – if the prospect already has one – for having bought the wrong sort. How the prospect reacts to this is unpredictable, and calls for a person-to-person dialogue to find out. (Hence, the worst sort of prospect is the tight-lipped, poker-faced type who hears the rep's presentation without comment, thus revealing nothing.) If Peter Drucker really did say, 'The purpose of marketing is to make selling redundant,'[3] he was wrong. Marketing can and should prepare the ground for sales activity, but whenever there is any serious, new product on the market, it will need *selling*, and the task will not be straight-forward.

One instinctive reaction to this assertion is to point out that there are plenty of professional buyers who select the merchandise found in shops. One might think they should be only too willing to try innovations, but the reality is not so. The success of the buyer tends to be judged by how well the products selected sell onwards to store customers. The tried and tested is therefore always preferable to the new and uncertain.This makes the rep's task even harder. Faced with a personal customer, it is possible to investigate and overcome objections, but if a professional buyer states 'my customers will not like it' what can the rep say, which does not call the buyer a liar? Such conservatism is not universal, and it varies from sector to sector, but overcoming the barrier often involves mutual self-help, with the rep discounting another product perhaps, or somehow guaranteeing the risk with the new one by offering to take it back if it does not sell. Even in rapidly evolving markets like electronics, a store may display – but not actually buy ahead until the demand is proven – the latest gizmo. For example, the pioneering Sinclair ZX80 kid's home computer had to be sold by mail order before store buyers woke up to the opportunity they were missing; the next year, there were 'stampedes' in certain shops when deliveries of the ZX81 versions arrived. Even people who own their own businesses, such as independent

---

[3] I saw this attribution to Drucker on an overhead slide in a lecture room; I wonder if the lecturer was in fact expressing his own opinion but sought to hide behind some greater authority.

fashion boutiques (and whom one might expect to be keen to buy according to their own preferences), respond to approaches from new suppliers with comments like, 'I have no budget', probably a blatant untruth inspired by paranoia. Approach them early for the next season, and what you get is, 'I don't know what my budget is yet.'

Feedback

This fear-of-failure phenomenon even extends to people actually in sales jobs. Those following regular calling rounds can be reluctant to ask for orders for new products, for fear of losing a sale elsewhere among the product range. To promote new products, manufacturers are obliged to use specialised freelance salesforces in competition with their own! The regular reps are merely 'order fillers' and not Heinz Goldman's creative salespeople. Selling, as Drucker did not say, but Goldman might have, only begins when the prospect says 'No'.

No matter how creative it may be, no sales manager would be pleased to run a force which came back empty-handed every day, insisting that they were capable salespeople, but that the prospects they were sent to call upon were unsuitable for the product. Once the salesforce is assigned, its job is to sell, yet a certain amount of screening or research is needed to ensure that the effort is well-directed. The question of whether the salesforce itself can help with this research is worth exploring.

There are big issues of motivation working in sales, and it is far from the truth to say that it always comes naturally to the people who are successful at it. A salesperson must first discover the prospect's objections – the prospect will naturally have objections, or start thinking of them – and then establish which are perceived, and can with skilful handling be removed, and which are real. Real objections can still be overcome, it is a matter of assessing the likely effort-return profile in trying to do so. Money is a further complication, since the ability to 'afford' something is in part subjective anyway. The answer, 'I would love a dishwasher but I have nowhere to put it,' is potentially a real objection, though if it comes at the beginning of a conversation, it could be a smoke screen. If it emerges after some time spent in conversation, should the rep accept it, or ask to see the kitchen? Once in the kitchen, are physical rearrangements possible? Can the clothes washer be relocated to the garage? How far should the rep take it? The next line of discovery could be that the prospect actually has no disposable income (and would have already bought a dishwasher in different circumstances), but is embarrassed to admit it. The space problem was an excuse.

Salesforce management

Deciding when to cut one's losses in a sales pitch is difficult, and the behaviour of individuals within a salesforce will depend upon the managerial, motivational and reward systems in force. These are often determined in part by peers, particularly where some concept of a collective 'ethical standard' is required. Appraising the results of a sales campaign is one of those topics which follows the 'uncertainty principle'. Are bad results a consequence of bad propositions, or bad methods of presentation? Usually, the emphasis is be placed on the latter, which is why sales training is a big industry. The striking implication is that most salespeople are not considered good at their jobs!

It can actually be very important to learn about customers' misperceptions in order to improve presentational ideas (citing yesterday's instead of tomorrow's bus being a case in point), but it is not for the creative seller to pause and sympathise with an objection which can be overcome. This is best left for the marketing department who should commission suitably organised qualitative research. It is clearly important to learn that it is a waste of time trying to sell dishwashers to people who live in caravans, for example, but such obvious basic screening should be done by whoever generates the leads, as they are called.

The question of how much time to spend on a particular prospect varies with the nature of the sale. If it is a single event, not to be repeated, then the overall cost of the salesforce can be divided by the contribution to be generated from the orders obtained, and some norms established. Commonly, the simplest way of regulating the reps' activity is by paying commission only; it is then up to the individuals to decide for themselves how to spent their time. In such circumstances, there is no requirement for the rep to establish anything other than a plausible, temporary need, which may prove to be spurious.

These sorts of situations are those which give selling a bad name, the case where the prospect will never account for more than one sale. In sharp contrast is the situation where the prospect will become, if all goes well, a regular customer, in which case, the subsequent value of the initial success could be substantial. Certainly, the rep should ensure that the sale is taking place for justifiable reasons, though not everybody sees it this way. Some sellers win temporary victories with undeliverable promises (presumably hoping that they personally will have moved on by the time the facts emerge). There are some 'precious' circumstances where the prospects number so few and are worth so much that the reps must never let the dialogue terminate; selling airliners is an obvious case. In fact, many business to business, relationship-based activities would fall into this category. Somewhere in between are the sales which are not repeated to an individual, but are subject to word of mouth reports, where the seller's reputation will have a bearing on future prospects. In these situations, selling can become an act of faith.

WHERE TO NEXT?

Service presents the added problem of selling an intangible (Chapter 8)

In the extreme case of the new venture, everything has to be sold (Chapter 12)

Sales effort cannot be capitalised, but should sometimes be regarded as an asset (Chapter 13)

Sales feedback is not a good form of research (Chapter 18)

Section 2

Turning activity into money

5. Pricing and profit contribution

Selling things for more money *than some target requires selling a certain volume at a given price. Changing the price changes the volume, which may change the target. What counts is the margin, not the money*

A cynic, said Oscar Wilde, is a man who knows the price of everything and the value of nothing. This is as witty a way as any of reminding us that value is something more than price. However, the price of something remains an integral part of what is offered for sale, the *total purchasing proposition*. Price is what in a business context distinguishes a product from an artefact – thus defining a product as something which changes hands commercially. How often have you admired something and expressed interest in buying it, only to lose that interest abruptly upon learning the price? Conversely, how many useless things do you own that you bought because they happened to be going cheap at the time?

With certain exceptions, the price of goods or services for sale is pre-determined by the business offering them. There are certain cultures in which final transaction prices are arrived at by extensive negotiating, bargaining, or haggling – to offer three levels of sophistication for what is essentially the same process – but the United Kingdom is not one of them.[1] It is true that the sales or relationship manager for the supplier may have reached some sort of financial agreement with the buyer or supply chain manager over future deliveries of an item in your supermarket, but if you take one of the said items to the checkout and attempt to bargain, people will think you are very strange. Given that the setting of prices is arguably the single most significant action in a business, it is remarkable how often decisions over prices are

[1] The antiques trade is a mysterious exception. There is a story of six dealers and one piece of furniture stranded on a desert island. With skilful trading, they all became millionaires.

taken casually or arbitrarily – and how infrequently any effort is made to adjust them after they are set.

Auctions

The major class of exceptions to pre-pricing is goods sold at auction, the principle of which is that the price continues to rise until only one of the people present is willing to pay the sum required. This system applies in the rarefied circumstance exemplified in Fine Art auctions where there is thought to be a demand for something, but no one really knows how much it is worth. In this situation, the price is what someone is prepared to pay, and Oscar was wrong really, for the value *is* the price.

The other circumstances where auctions apply are at the opposite end of the scale, where they are used to set the short-term price of commodities. Here people try to pay as little as possible to obtain what they need. Overall, their actions are regulated by how strongly they want something – a concept broadly known as utility in economics – and how much of it is available. The existence of the utility concept acknowledges that Oscar was right, and price is not everything. How much they finally pay is also determined by how much others are prepared to bid. The classic British auction perhaps contains an element of cynicism, with people persistently trying to get away with bidding much less than they are prepared to pay. A Dutch auction operates differently, with the price declining until someone decides it is fair for what is on offer and 'stops the clock'.

The auction process exemplifies a basic principle, namely that for most things offered for sale, the higher the price, the fewer the people willing to pay it. This is not always true – there are some things for which a higher price may increase its desirability (notably luxury items such as perfume), and there are some things for which a higher price will result in no sales at all. The latter are called commodities, such as sand, or ready-mixed concrete. Provided the buyer actually knows the price of more than one supplier, there should be no reason not to buy the cheapest. For this condition to apply, all other things have to be equal. There has to be a regularity of supply, otherwise availability outstrips price as the reason for buying. This used to be the case in the centrally-planned economy of the USSR where people would carry 'perhaps bags' with them when not shopping, just in case they came across something available to buy.

Demand schedules

Relationships between alternative prices and the numbers of willing buyers are features of the market system, and the specific pattern between the volume of goods the market is willing to purchase and the price is known as the *demand curve or schedule*. In economics, quantity is shown on the horizontal or x axis, which would normally imply it to be the independent variable. Economists then introduce the concept of *elasticity*, which is the rate at which a change in *price* is reflected in a proportionate change in *quantity* – implying quantity is the dependent variable. Proportionate measures are used to ensure that the scales on which price and quantity are counted are comparable. Finally, because usually an increase in price results in a decrease in quantity and vice versa the expression is given a minus sign. If this is as clear as mud, never mind.[2] The fact is that – at any given point in time – a situation exists in which different numbers of people will buy different quantities of something, according to the price set. If the price is not pre-set, it will be determined at a rate which equates the available supply to this demand schedule.

Things are much more interesting when the price is pre-set, because this is commonly the case in business. (It is true that in the long run, quantity determines price for manufactured goods in the sense that prices decline over time with volume increases, but sometimes early pricing decisions mean that goods fail to make it to mass production levels.) Sellers who are aware of the demand curve they face are in a position to set prices such that they exactly sell out of their stock, or so that they obtain from the market the maximum revenue it will provide. It is thus a very useful concept, except that unfortunately it is very difficult to establish the demand curve exactly, because it is often apparent only *after* prices have been set. In physical markets selling fruit

---

[2] The mathematical expression for demand elasticity is

$$\frac{-y}{x} \cdot \frac{dx}{dy}$$

where the x axis measures quantity, and the y axis price.

and vegetables, you can watch people working out the demand curve as the day progresses. Often it is done by experience; consumers have been known to complain that shopkeepers unfairly raise the price of brussels sprouts at Christmas, for example. In fact, the raised price means that either people buy fewer sprouts than they would otherwise, or fewer people buy sprouts at all. Thus, the available quantity 'goes further'. This is not a trick; it is the market system at work.

Price changes

If you were running a business, and you knew how your demand schedule worked, what would you do to your prices? According to economists, you would seek to maximise profits. In part, this behaviour can actually be observed, if only by default, as businesses can be seen to discontinue unprofitable activities. Theoretically, the concept of profit maximisation derives from motives of rational expectations which in reality do not represent the full picture. With purely rational motives, few people would end up running businesses for themselves. Nevertheless, maximising profits remains a definite option, and profits are certainly something that investors in business like to see.

To discuss the effects of price changes, we need to examine some numbers. Consider the case of a village shop (or a neighbourhood convenience store) which is unable to compete on price with supermarkets, and therefore trades on other factors such as locality, hours of business, service, bus routes etc. Would the shopkeeper benefit from raising or lowering prices? This is not a trivial question – people have been known to invest large redundancy payments in buying shops, only to lose much of it through poor pricing decisions.

The instinctive argument goes like this: 'Lowering prices will increase the number of customers coming to the store, and more customers must be a good thing.' The first part of this is correct, but from a profit perspective, the second part is not proven.

Suppose that the shop normally sells 100 cans of baked beans in the course of a week at the recommended retail price of say 40p. Normally, the shopkeeper will buy at a discount of between 25% and 28%, so the cost price of the beans is 29p per can, say. The local shop will not sell in sufficient volume to buy direct from a manufacturer, and may well find that a local supermarket is actually offering a price lower than 29p, so sales will be essentially dependent on non-price factors. Suppose further that a price decrease of 10% will result in a 20% increase in volume, and that a 10% increase in price will result in a 20% decline. These factors are speculative, but everything else can be deduced.

(We are discussing a general pricing policy, with everything in the shop being priced above or below recommended levels as the case may be, using the example of baked beans to demonstrate a general principle. We are not dealing with the idea of making an exception of baked beans, on the theory that customers will come into the shop specifically to buy cheap baked beans, and while they are there, get the rest of their shopping.[3] The volume changes are forecast to occur abruptly, and it is recognised that in the event the pattern of customer behaviour will take a while to settle down. It will take a time for people to realise that the prices are low, and high prices will initially discourage people who will 'drift back' as it becomes convenient. Under consideration therefore is the shopkeeper's long-term strategy, not a short-term tactic.)

In financial terms, what is important to the shopkeeper is not the revenue, but the profit generated in each sale. The gross profit equation for a food retailer is simple, being the selling price minus the cost price per item, assuming no perishability or problems with 'best before' dates. At the MRP, profit on a can of beans is 40p – 29p = 11p. The shopkeeper sees 40p, but only keeps 11p; the other 29p goes to replace the can.

Consider then the three scenarios:

	Selling price	**Cost price**	**Gross profit**	**Volume per week**	**Takings per week**	**Profit per week**
MRP	40p	29p	11p	100	£40	£11
Low price option (LPO)	36p	29p	7p	120	£43.20	£8.40
High price option (HPO)	44p	29p	15p	80	£35.20	£12

[3] This is the 'loss leader' concept, which does not work. See Chapter 9.

The shopkeeper who judges performance by counting the takings (and most of them do, most of the time, up to and including retailers in the FTSE 100) will be delighted with the low price option, but the winner is clearly the high price option, which earns more money for less effort. Compared to the HPO, the LPO involves 50% more sales (120 versus 80) which represents considerably more work fetching and carrying etc, and may actually compound the error by increasing the overheads of the shop to cope with the extra activity.

Of course, if this increase in trade enables the shopkeeper to renegotiate the cost price, the situation changes. It was this scenario that Joseph Cohen, the founder of Tesco, had in mind when he adopted the motto 'pile it high, sell it cheap'. What he meant was 'buy it cheap'!

You can actually work out that the cost price would need to fall to 26p – marginally more than 10% – for the LPO to deliver the same profit as the HPO, and still operating costs would remain higher. The margin for the wholesaler supplying the retailer is probably around 10%, so obtaining the required discount would have to involve trading direct with the manufacturer. The latter would find the bother of transacting too costly.

It is acknowledged that a neighbourhood shopkeeper may have other factors to consider besides pricing policy and maximising profits, not the least of which is that many customers are also neighbours, with whom a friendly relationship may be desirable. Village shops are sometimes considered to have a community focus and responsibility – for example, to notice when an elderly person has not been seen recently – but if so, perhaps the community has a reciprocal obligation to trade at the store at its prices. The general significance of this financial conclusion is that earnings from trading goods bought for a fixed price are determined by the *margin*, but the discount is calculated on the *price*. Hence, a 10% discount on a 40p can of beans which has a gross profit of 11p is actually a reduction of four-elevenths or 36% in the retailer's income, which puts the calculations into perspective.

Prices and volumes

Things are different in a manufacturing context. What something costs to make is a more complex – and debatable –

consideration. Basic principles of costing are discussed elsewhere, but the difference is that there are various expenses incurred in running a factory, whether it operates at its maximum capacity or not, which are included in the cost of the products. A price reduction may make sense if it secures additional volumes which would not otherwise be produced. As demand grows, bigger factories may be built, and provided they reach target volumes, products have lower average costs, while producers can still earn bigger profits.

At a strategic level, decisions about prices and their impact on volumes are very important. Sometimes, prices can be driven down as new entrants into a market compete on price in order to secure any distribution at all, or perhaps – in the case of high technology – have a later generation of components and therefore a lower cost threshold for a given volume. Competing firms are forced to lower prices or lose sales (that is how it looks anyway) and so they try to obtain further economies of manufacturing scale to support a lower cost base. This is typically what happens with consumer durables, where appliances move from low volume, luxury status, and the price declines as they become high volume necessities.

There is generally a choice between maximising *contribution* (another term for gross profit, which also allows for the marketing costs directly associated with the sales generated) and maximising *revenue*, which tends to happen when firms are more interested in market share than profit. According to economic theory, the course followed which allows for cost variations should be to sell at ever decreasing prices until marginal revenue equals marginal cost. In practice, this can be very difficult if not impossible to do. If customers who have paid full price find out about those who paid marginal prices, they can become very annoyed even though they were originally quite happy. Once again, the irrational side of human behaviour takes over. Another difficulty in following the theory is that as previously stated, the demand schedule may not be evident until prices are quoted and customer reaction obtained.

There are few circumstances in which a firm would voluntarily choose to lower prices. Without competition, such as when the product is protected by a patent, the profit maximising choice should prevail, except in circumstances where the item being sold generates a basis for further sales, such as with a proprietary camera and its film, or in the penetration of compact disc players, which then opened up the market for recorded discs themselves. In the early days of domestic VCRs, publishers of recorded videotapes looked at the number of households with video players, decided it was small, and set correspondingly high prices for their pre-recorded videotapes of movies etc, hoping to make a profit from small volumes. This short-sighted approach immediately created markets both for pirated tapes, and for rentals, both of which reduced the publishers' sales and continued to do so as VCR ownership spread. It is only some fifteen years later that publishers are finally trying to encourage people to collect videotapes, something that has always been the norm for books and music, and might have been from the start of video had there been more far-sighted pricing policies.

Premium pricing

When there is competition, and it is active, one of the major objectives of marketing activity is actually to secure a premium price for the product, even though it also sells in high volumes. This is the objective of *branding*. The marketing costs have to be added into the contribution equation before it can be said to be worth doing – and often it is not, since by definition, not everything can be a premium brand. When it is successful, however, branding confounds normal demand curves. The successful brand is bought by more people, more often, at an above-average price.

When competition is expected to appear in due course and a single firm has a lead, there is a choice, known in marketing circles as either *skimming the cream*, or maximising *penetration*. The former policy is roughly about profit maximising for as long as competitors allow; the latter is used where the objective is to create repeat purchase patterns, brand loyalty, or to open distribution channels. The product is priced to maximise sales volumes, subject to basic profitability assumptions. Distributors normally operate on standard margins (a percentage of total revenue), so they may take a different view about the preferred strategy anyway – they require high turnover to stock the product at all. For many consumer goods, retailers' cooperation is essential, so the pricing options need to be examined accordingly. For a new product, the opening price says quite a lot about it, and it is important in test marketing that prices are used which reflect the final strategy, even if this means selling at a loss in the short term. One of the weaknesses of test markets is that if they don't work, is it the product, or the price at fault? It is probably better to undertake product trials where people use it without having to pay, and to use free samples to promote trial purchases.

Some manufacturers effectively override the law which prohibits the fixing of retail prices by printing special packs with a price in large type, challenging the retailers to try and sell at a different price. Independents have no choice but to accept these packs if they are all that is available, and with them the likelihood of reduced margins because the manufacturer has decided unilaterally that the distributors will 'participate' in the consumer promotion (that is, the manufacturer has reduced the retail price, but left the wholesale price unaltered). This does not happen with the chain supermarkets, whose buying power tends to dominate. The issue is much more likely to be about whether the manufacturer will also supply goods under the store's own label.

Price rises

Part of the reason firms are reluctant to experiment with price rises is that it is generally thought that it is not then possible to lower them again. Few therefore investigate the opportunities provided by the 'other side' of the demand schedule. In fact, there are some notable occasions when prices have been raised successfully, though it is usually one of several actions which disguise the impact somewhat. The example of Perrier is a case in point. There was a publicity scare about levels of benzene in Perrier water which caused its withdrawal from the UK market, until it was established that the benzene level was actually less than that occurring in other natural sources. It was then relaunched, at a similar price to its previous level. The difference was that what had formerly been one-litre bottles were now only 75 centilitres.

In the more obscure markets occupied by specialist firms, often small or medium sized, there may be plenty of opportunities to raise prices, such as when a component is being supplied which has a high performance specification but is relatively low value in the end product. Provided there is an ostensible reason, a price rise is not a problem. An engineering firm may find itself also working on government contracts where a low price is deemed to be important – but in return, that customer is prepared to wait for delivery. There is definitely a case supporting an alternative pricing strategy for industrial customers for whom time might be of the essence. We are in fact reasonably used to multiple pricing for air and rail travel, for example, where there is a marginal difference in 'quality' or class of the ticket.

It is not uncommon for firms to attract custom they do not want! People will insist that they do not make any money out of certain customers because of the fuss they create, or the small size of orders involved, yet they dare not raise the price for fear of losing the custom. In an extreme case, I once encountered a firm which would have sold its whole output at a loss had it reached capacity, but claimed its (sole) customer would not consider a price rise. Such attitudes may stem from the adage 'the customer is always right' but like the modification needed to the 'pile it high, sell it cheap' slogan, this should perhaps read 'the *profitable* customer is always right'. If there are genuinely unprofitable customers there is nothing to be lost from raising the price; either they refuse to pay it, in which case the losses are removed, or they do pay it, and become profitable.

In the early days of Britain's membership of the European Union, UK wholesalers (not the manufacturers) of 'Johnnie Walker Red Label' whisky invoked the Treaty of Rome to prevent the manufacturer banning them from re-selling the whisky in continental Europe. Outside the UK, it commanded a premium price – but this was the result of the manufacturer's investment in branding, the benefits of which it wished to keep for itself.[4] Defeated in the courts, the manufacturer withdrew the brand from the UK market – a decision appearing to imply that UK consumers would not tolerate a price rise. Yet, if the alternative was withdrawal, there would have been nothing to lose by trying it. A few years later, it was relaunched with the slogan 'Johnnie is back', but this time at a premium price by UK standards, as if expecting that consumers would remember the name but not the price. As we know, consumers are not stupid,

---

[4] This is a very clear case of the price being part of the total purchasing proposition. The contents of UK and European bottles were identical.

and 'JW Red' never achieved its former sales volumes, though whether it contributed profits as a premium brand similar to those before its withdrawal, only the manufacturer knows.

If there are circumstances where a price rise can be tested on a sample of customers, it should be. If there is no repeat purchasing involved, such as with some kind of emergency or special need, say key cutting, window replacement, etc, sales volume can be monitored to see whether a price rise appears to deter potential customers. If customers are not repeat buyers, or if they are but they do not talk to each other (because of geographical separation for example), there are possibilities. If the decision is made to adopt premium pricing, then it is necessary to live with the consequences, which will probably take the form of complaints. There is a general store near Paddington in west London which is open 24 hours daily, 365 (or 366!) days per year.[5] After midnight, the price of every item is increased by a fixed sum; when inexperienced customers complain, the checkout cashier just puts the offending item to one side and serves the next customer. It is not worth arguing, and people who want to shop after midnight learn that they must pay for the privilege.

The need for numbers

There is a story by Somerset Maugham about the verger of a church who loses his job because he cannot read or write, only to develop a chain of successful tobacconists. Upon discovering his customer's illiteracy, the bank manager's reaction is to ask what would have happened if he had had a proper education, to which the subject replies that he would still be the verger. It is entertaining, if implausible to imagine that a chain of shops could run without paperwork (or its electronic substitute). What is certain is that no one – however much they dislike arithmetic – can afford to ignore numbers in business. As long as things have to be sold for more money than is spent in so doing, there is a need to count, add, and subtract. Percentages also creep in from time to time, and although there is a good parallel between percentage and pence in the pound, there is a source of possible

[5] It literally never closes: it is physically open on to the street, and does not have a door!

confusion over two methods of relating the selling price of something to its cost, namely *margin* and *mark-up*.

The *margin* is the profit element *expressed as a percentage of the selling price*. It is used in retailing when the goods are sold at a recommended price, and bought cheaper. The amount of discount on the selling price is the same as the margin. In the baked beans example, cans selling for 40p are bought at a discount of 11p each, giving a margin of eleven-fortieths, or 27.5%. More generally margin is used to calculate the profit element when the price is set for reasons unrelated directly to the cost. Margin ranges between 0% (no profit on the transaction) to 100% (no cost element in what is sold).

Mark-up is what a retailer adds to a cost price to obtain a selling price, and is the profit element *expressed as a percentage of the cost price*. It has no limits, therefore, other than what the customer is willing to pay. A mark-up of 400% means adding four times the cost to the cost itself to obtain the selling price. Something bought for £2 and marked-up 400% would thus sell for £2+£8 = £10. Mark-up is common in department store retailing where a pre-determined percentage is applied to cost prices as a general policy. (It also occurs widely in service and contracting businesses where costs are estimated and a percentage added 'for overheads and profit'.) A mark-up of 150% would add a profit of £2×150% = £3 to the cost of £2, giving a price of £5.

If ever you are involved in setting or interpreting prices, it is vitally important to understand which method is being used. If it is over 100%, it must be a mark-up, but people readily confuse the two terms by talking of, for example, 100% profit. This could just be a 100% margin, in the very unlikely event that the goods were obtained for nothing, but it is more likely to be a mark-up (it is also a fairly common percentage to use). A 100% mark-up yields a price of twice the cost; the profit element must be the same as the cost, therefore, so it is half the selling price, or 50%. If someone talks of a 50% profit, beware; does it mean a 50% margin – and 100% mark-up as just calculated, or is it a 50% mark-up? Putting a 50% mark-up on something which cost £2 would mean adding £1. The selling price would be £3, and the margin one-third or roughly 33%. Make sure you spot the difference.

WHERE TO NEXT?

Price levels can be raised using advertising (Chapter 2)
The loss leader concept is a mistaken (Chapter 9)
Price volatility has a dramatic effect on high gearing (Chapter 15)
Forecasting helps with understanding price options (Chapter 17)

6. The nature and quality of operations

Businesses can choose to concentrate on their ability to ***sell things repeatedly*** *to best effect, or to limit the* ***money that is spent in so doing****, but not normally both*

When Michael Heseltine became Deputy Prime Minister, a press conference explained how duties would be divided between John Major and his new deputy. One of the responsibilities to appear on the latter's list was for 'the efficiency and effectiveness of government departments'. Asked to explain what this was, a spokesperson replied with words to the effect that 'efficiency is doing things right, effectiveness is doing the right things.' Answers of this nature are probably applauded in political circles, for they sound impressive but represent no commitment to a single course of action. This is absolutely the last thing one wants to hear in business (though this same description can be found in management development texts), where the course of action is everything. Indeed, possibly the greatest dilemma to be found in business development occurs when information from the marketplace shows that a plan is not working. The question is always, 'Is it because what we are doing is not right, or because we are not doing it the right way?'

Along with their lesser known cousins *Economy* and *Excellence, Efficiency* and *Effectiveness* are in fact strategic terms that describe the way a business orientates itself towards providing customer satisfaction along three broad dimensions of cost, quality and availability. Essentially, *effectiveness* implies always being able to supply a customer, *efficiency* is always achieving a budgeted cost. Once the decision is taken to supply customers using one strategy, this can be assumed to be correct (unless customers indicate otherwise). It should then be clear how to 'do things right' once the 'things' that need doing have been defined by the strategic choice.

E-strategies

Effectiveness and efficiency can be likened to having market or manufacturing orientations, but there is no need for anything physical to be made for the choice to be a consideration. As operational strategies, they may also be employed in non-financial circumstances, but the impact in business is of course their effect on profits.

For example, an *efficient* public transport system would be one which obtained the lowest cost per passenger. This would entail large capacity buses running at lengthy intervals; passengers would have to wait, but the buses would run mostly full. An *effective* system is one which maximises the number of passengers carried. Small buses running at frequent intervals mean short waits, a policy which encourages people to use them, and benefits all. This fact has been recognised by transport authorities and overnight courier firms, but not yet by transporters of their own goods, judging by the ever-increasing size of vehicles used on delivery runs. (Note the potential confusion; in everyday language, people might talk of an efficient bus service, actually meaning effective.)

On a personal note, in the days when I spent much time lecturing, I used my Christmas bonus one year to buy several shirts of different colours. The idea was to increase the choice available each day – an effectiveness strategy. My wife, who did the laundry, saw things differently and allowed unwashed shirts of each main colour to accumulate until an efficient batch size (expressed in washing machine loads) was obtained. Thus my strategy of choice became 'this week it's blue'; I could have changed this by taking over the laundry duties, but somehow I never did.

An interesting business example is from the hand knitting needle industry. If it seems an obscure choice, remember that over 50 per cent of women and some men have at some time been hand knitters (though the practice may finally be declining for ever). This makes knitting as big a volume activity as most DIY sectors, and someone has to supply the needles. In any case, it is worth recording that strategies apply in all businesses, however specialised or obscure; sometimes, scope limits the options for very small companies, which makes them rather uninteresting.

The two British needle manufacturers produced similar

products, at similar prices. Interestingly, different sized needles bore different prices (and some used different materials) suggesting that the prices were derived from the cost of manufacture. One of the things which would change between a 3.25mm and a 4mm needle was the amount of steel required, and the 4mm version was more expensive. It appeared from the pattern of deliveries that a manufacturing-efficient policy was adopted to control this cost. Probably, different sizes were scheduled for manufacture in long runs, thus reducing downtime in changing over sizes. Production quantities would probably be forecast from last year's sales. This appeared to be a satisfactory policy, as both manufacturers regularly sold their total production. Some of the above is supposition concluded after the event, but the last point is certainly true, as there were circumstances when they would regularly sell out of certain sizes. Manufacturing management may have regarded this as prudent; unfilled orders would be held over until a new batch was produced. Customers were a few department stores and large numbers of small retailers; the occasional stock-out would not bother them unduly.

Seen from the customer's point of view, this approach failed to maximise the opportunities. Starting from an analysis of the behaviour of the consumer (as all business issues should be approached) certain things can be said about the purchase of a pair of knitting needles. Firstly, the size is determined by the yarn and pattern to be knitted. There is no prospect of someone buying a smaller size because they are cheaper, so the price of the various other sizes is irrelevant. Maintaining different prices just adds a complication for the retailer. Secondly, the needles are almost certainly being purchased along with the yarn to be knitted, and represent only a proportion of the total expenditure, so the consumer is not overly sensitive to price. In that case, there is no particular need for the manufacturer to strive for the lowest cost.

It is the third aspect of the purchase which is critical. There is a very good chance that the consumer already possesses a pair of the correct size if only they can be located. This is a big 'if' however, and, being keen to get home and start the project, many knitters will tend to include the correct needles with their purchase 'just in case'. Of course, if the retailer is out of stock (because the manufacturer is), the sale will not take place, and may well be lost for ever. The enthusiastic knitter goes home and locates or borrows a pair. Individually, this is only one small sale, but the collective effect is considerable, as these extra sales would go straight to the manufacturers' – and the retailers' – bottom line. For those in the industry, it is not trivial. During the last great hand knitting 'boom' every autumn would see a switch to knitting for school wear, and the whole country would run out of size 5.5mm knitting needles. As the shopkeepers failed to make these sales, they would not order extra needles after the event, so there was no feedback to the manufacturers about what had actually happened. Thus, they carried on believing they were eventually fulfilling all their orders.

Knitting needles are one of those peculiar categories of product, like combs and pens, which continue to sell long after the marketplace should be saturated. One imagines that it was not out of a sense of the public good that the sales were 'declined' by the manufacturers, however. There is a more general point, that if all the knitters had actually been obliged to wait to buy the needles before they could start knitting, this would result in some idleness and lost capacity for the 'industry' as a whole. This is undesirable on a macro or national scale; it was a common occurrence in the last days of central planning in the USSR, when production in one place would be held up completely for want of a simple component which was not seen as a priority elsewhere. There are many more complex or sophisticated industries where profits do not derive from the sale of original equipment, but rather the aftermarket of spares and service, where a policy of effectiveness – always being able to supply the customer – is required. It may cost more, but this is more than compensated by increased revenues.

Sticking to the subject of knitting,[1] an important factor in Benetton's success selling sweaters has been the policy of garment dyeing. The traditional, efficient method of producing coloured sweaters is to dye the fibres, spin them into yarn, and knit them. A less efficient approach is to dye the yarn, but this is still better (cheaper) from a manufacturing perspective than dying the knitted article. The secret of being effective on the other hand is to get the colour mix right through each fashion season, with the aim of never being out of stock of the best sellers, and not being overstocked with less popular colours to

---

[1] The expression 'sticking to your knitting' has its own meaning in a business strategy context. See Chapter 11.

the extent that they have to be marked down in price at the end of the season. Manufacturing cycles mean that colour forecasts have to be made ahead of the season's start.

Benetton solved this problem by retaining 10 per cent of their stock undyed (known in Italian as *grigio*). The effectiveness of this 'inefficient' process was – and is – superb, as it provides time to react each season, something which could not be done through knitting because the machines are already in use for next season, and a re-order process would probably take too long anyway. The extra cost of dyeing the sweaters made as *grigio* is clearly compensated for by their selling for a full profit contribution instead of being cleared out at a small loss.

Strategic choice

The choice of an effectiveness or an efficiency strategy is really a matter of computing the costs and benefits of both and making a decision. What does not work is opting for one and trying to do the other, and each may result in some forgone sales, either because the price is too high, or the delivery is too slow.

In a mass market with predictable patterns of demand, it is more likely that efficiency will be the route to choose, but it also depends on who in the supply chain holds the greatest sway. *Just In Time* manufacturing strategies where the production flow lines of a component supplier and its assembler customer are coordinated to the extent that components travel directly into trucks for delivery straight on to the assembler's line are examples where efficiency *and* effectiveness are found together. This may be achieved through the careful sharing of information, and it is in one sense anti-competitive since the parties are locked into a relationship – a *strategic partnership* – which is difficult to break. Provided flow lines can be designed so that one exactly feeds the other, there is the compensation of genuine economic benefit from the system; if not, and one firm wants to supply the other's components, it has no choice but to hold stocks and deliver as required, never minding the cost. In fact, it may subcontract the delivery; one of the beneficiaries of JIT systems is the logistics industry.

If the two Es of efficiency and effectiveness approximate to trading off cost against availability, implicit within this is an assumption about quality. In fact, this can also be varied, giving rise to another pair of strategies: *Excellence*, where the quality is so incomparable that the customer will wait and then still pay a high price, and *Economy*, where things are cheap and available and, consequently, not up to much. There are plenty of circumstances where economy is a sensible strategy, such as in mass market fashions. Every season brings an uncertainty about exactly which of a range of styles and colours (as in the Benetton example) will capture the imagination. The younger fashion-conscious consumers do not have large amounts of money to spend, and will not wear this season's clothes again, but they want 'the look', and they want it quickly. Excellence is the strategy pursued by the rock stars and other celebrities these consumers idolise, if you care to regard them as businesses (and you can bet their managers do).

Operations management

Operations management is the term which is given – in the context of *Understanding Business* – to the control of 'it' – that which a business actually does or has which its customers are willing to pay for. It is not therefore limited to production management, though it may in many instances be taken as a synonym. E-strategies – efficiency, effectiveness, et al – are points on a spectrum of ideal operational configurations. In theory, for any given strategy, an operational set-up can be established, which it is then a matter of routine to manage. The design of the system is obviously critical to any strategic decision, since the manner in which something is produced affects its cost (and thence the parameters for its price), its quality, and its availability or delivery. In practice, things are not so straightforward because customers do not all subscribe to a similar profile. In an environment of different products selling at different speeds requiring different output rates or capacities, operations management is a complex subject.

As a general principle, if a business is operating in the loombucket manufacturing industry, it should be a safe assumption that it is actually capable of producing loombuckets, so it should not be beyond its technical staff to lay out proposals for alternative investment strategies which will offer, say, the lowest cost per item, or the fastest response time, for a board of directors to contemplate. Much in the operations sphere tends to be of a technical nature, which makes it difficult to generalise and unsuitable for extensive coverage here. This is not to suggest that it is unimportant; much business success stems from achievement in the operations sphere, particularly in service businesses, in meeting unpredictable, unexpected, and sometimes unreasonable demands from customers. Old hands in industry may claim that it is the job of marketing to find customers for what operations can supply. A more enlightened view advocates the reverse. Either way, there tends to be a tension between operations and marketing or sales, in which production people usually have the whip-hand in terms of saying what can and can't be done. That requires technical knowledge, whereas anyone can comment on what customers can and can't do. Things do not have to be so technical for problems to arise in services, as anyone who has been the other side of the kitchen door in a restaurant will recognise.

Perhaps these difficulties stem from human factors, which contribute to the frequent separation of production into a distinct subcontracting business, particularly in areas of greater uncertainty such as fashion, electronics, media, etc. It is usually thought that manufacturing subcontractors are based in different parts of the world from their marketing customers because of differences in labour costs, but this may not be the only, or even the most important, reason. Japan's and Germany's labour costs have never been particularly low in absolute terms in the last thirty years, and they have risen persistently because of the continued appreciation of their currencies, yet they are two successful 'manufacturing' nations. Meanwhile, Marks & Spencer's suppliers remain predominantly British, seemingly competing successfully with counterparts in lower cost countries. Perhaps the reason is that firms operating in less developed economies are prepared to accept the relative certainty of a small margin on a full order book – a normal profit in return for continuous work – as opposed to a super profit from a dominant market position.

Concentration into suitable manufacturing units enables firms to specialise on one of the E-strategies. It does not explain how the subcontract Japanese firms operate who supply, for example, their motor industry and appear to help ride out recessions, but it is easy to see how a typical firm will fill up its order book with efficiency-based quotes until delivery dates get out of hand, while another will wait around, apparently short of work, until a last minute order is received which, by nature of its urgency, can command a premium price. Operations in small firms can take on a flexibility which makes them difficult to analyse systematically, but then the flow of work into the firm (the starting point for any analysis) is not usually so complex that it cannot be evaluated on its immediate merits. There are two significant issues, *capacity* and *scheduling*.

Capacity constraints

Capacity is not static but a dynamic measure, referring to what a system can produce per day or other unit of time. In any sequence of multiple tasks, there is always one which represents the *capacity constraint*, or bottleneck, unless the system is a continuous flow line. As the pattern of orders changes, so the location of the constraint can change of its own accord, but a reasonable human brain can usually notice this and take action, provided the constraint is adjustable. Relieving the constraint from one position shifts it to another, and further judgment is needed accordingly. If constraints are adjusted by moving people between different activities, the apparently logical conclusion will be that the least constrained configuration is one where everyone is equally busy. For long runs, this converts to an efficiency strategy. The correct number of people and/or machines are employed at each stage of the process for the work to flow smoothly from start to finish. This is the basic principle of manufacturing economies of scale. For short-term tasks, keeping everyone busy is like having 'all hands to the pumps'. It is effectiveness at work.

Consider the cafeteria in a motorway service station. At off-peak times, the cashier will sometimes be idle, and at the hot food counter, the chef will provide certain things – fried eggs, for example – to order. If there is a queue, it will be here, at the fried eggs. At busier times, the chef will fry eggs in anticipation, and the queues will be found at the checkout. At this point, another till will be opened, possibly shifting the bottleneck to the hot drinks counter. (This was common when drinks were served by the cup. The method of pots and *cafetières* not only increases the revenue, it also speeds the flow.) One Friday evening peak time, I arrived at the restaurant which was short of a cashier. It was chaos and, from a business perspective, unforgivable as sales were being lost when potential customers saw the queues and turned away. The egg-fryer was perplexed: there were more than enough fried eggs, and nothing therefore to do. The answer would have been for the chef to do a quick spell on the till and relieve the backlog. This would have happened in a privately run business such as a pub, notwithstanding any difficulties about hygiene, uniforms, and actually closing the till down again to fry more eggs. Presumably, under the rules of the organisation running the restaurant the egg-fryer was not trained, permitted, or instructed to operate the till. Of course, the manager could also have worked the till – but there was no sign of a manager.

Having a group of generalist, versatile staff is a more expensive option – they need more training, and are not perhaps as good at providing specialised efficiencies – but they deliver a more adaptable, effective business.

Schedules

The order in which the workload is *scheduled* affects the location and adjustment of capacity constraints, and is historically a skilled job where calculation is useful but experience probably more so, particularly in environments where the speed of carrying out the work is not entirely predictable. Computing facilities make possible the calculation of preferences on a statistical basis which would, under manual systems, have left the production line idle for weeks while a result was calculated. Judgmental factors still remain, for there will be times where perfection is unachievable – and mathematical optimisation schemes can only work if there is some ordinal system for comparing possible results. Each outcome must be either preferable or deferrable to every other, a situation not easily programmable if there is a prospect of say a) rushing a prototype and risking the quality of what might be a 'big chance' with a speculative new customer, b) being late with a large regular order for a big customer which might have a slight financial penalty but won't lose the business, or c) doing a 'special job' for the charity run by the Chairman's wife? Comparing alternatives, one can imagine that the big chance (a) should come before the regular order (b), while the Chairman's wife's charity work (c) can wait for the big order (b) to be cleared, but who dare tell the

Chairman's wife that her charity (c) is lower priority than a speculative little job (a) for a firm which is not even a regular customer? In other words, (a) before (b), and (b) before (c), but (c) before (a). How the manager copes with this (a computer can't) may depend on the reward system in force!

In a small firm, the manager is usually the owner, and there is a big choice to be made (in theory at least) between growing the business, and maximising profits at the current level. As the order book fills up, so the workload will start to reach capacity at places or for periods of time, beyond which orders should not be accepted as they compromise the firm's E-strategy, either through late delivery, rushed and therefore poor quality work, or overtime which must be charged at a higher price. Leaving space to operate normally creates an amount of 'slack' in the system which, if market conditions permit, may be sold off to a different sort of customer on a very different basis. A printing company with regular production of quality magazines might use its machines for telephone directories for which cost, but not time, are important. Orders in this second category can be accepted only up to total capacity, and the firm gets the maximum for what it can do, but it cannot pursue more business from its mainstream market. If it has the latter objective, it should find a way of expanding capacity and ignore the second customer group.

The practical problem with the maximisation strategy is that the people doing the actual work have to have considerable mental agility to know when they should take time and care, and when to bash the work out. Imagine how much complexity this would create in a large firm where not only people but capital equipment would be required to 'point in two directions at once'. There are some industries where this simply cannot be done, such as with automobiles, where operational set-ups for all but the smallest manufacturers are unable to cope with severe downturns in demand.

Quality standards

In the last ten years, firms throughout Britain have sometimes volunteered and often been obliged to obtain a certificate under the ISO 9000 series of the European Union (or its predecessor, the British 5750). It should be noted that previous non-possession of a certificate would not imply poor quality. In the shape of appearance, function, longevity, etc, basically the firm's customers made those decisions. Improving most of these against some absolute standard would not make any difference to trade provided it did not affect cost; the end user or consumer would be the principal beneficiary, for in the eyes of the firm's customers, the improvements should be unnecessary. The exception to this is longevity, since making a longer lasting loombucket would tend to reduce the overall size of the replacement market. Quality improvements are usually a competitive tactic, and not as in this case, something that happens across the board. On the other hand, quality changes which increase cost and therefore price would affect customer relationships, probably terminally.

So, the ISO standards are not about the quality[2] of the output so much as the process by which it is achieved. If the consequence means involving all employees in a better understanding of their employer's overall objectives and thence their own priorities, they are to be applauded. If, however, they imply restricting human capability by documenting every procedure (and this is the basic design of these particular standards) then the originators of the schemes should first examine their own concepts of quality, for the approach belongs to another century (and it is not the twenty-first). Any well-run business should already have its own systems and procedures which should be translatable into an ISO without much difficulty, but with a certain waste of time. Any business without any implicit systems either should not survive long enough to count (since it will not retain its customers), or is making a lot of mistakes which are costing it money. Here the Standard might help, but one has to ask what the management was doing to allow the mistakes in the first place (and for that matter, what extra costs does it incur in avoiding them). Rather as the existence of a Human Resource Department may permit in badly-managed firms the state of mind that managers do not have responsibility for their subordinates as humans, having a Department of Quality might imply that line managers do not need to include quality in their list of responsibilities. This is not desirable.

---

[2] In fairness, Standards do not necessarily use the word 'quality'. For example, ISO 9001 provides a 'Certificate of Registration of a Firm of Assessed Capability'.

It has been said that British attitudes to quality have been brought into line with expectations for the twenty-first century by the ISO series. There is a probably apocryphal story of the Japanese firm which responded to the reliability specification 'two parts per million oversized' with the request to be excused the production of the two oversized parts as they were proving very difficult to make. There is the true story of the British lawyer who was criticised in some quarters of the Gulf expatriate community for acting for a local State against a British company working on an order for aircraft. The planes had been ordered for use on the local runway (n metres long) but they required n + 200 metres to take off. The lawyer was thought to be acting in an 'un-British' manner in complaining. So, if the ISO effect is to make British managers more aware of quality, it is somewhat ironic that it started life as a British Standard.

WHERE TO NEXT?

Selling promises should reflect operational strategy (Chapter 4)
The rest of the organisation must follow any quality principles (Chapter 11)
Depreciation of plant etc should match strategic expectations (Chapter 13)
Success requires feedback, which requires an information flow (Chapter 19)

7. How much do things cost?

The business equation concerns ***money spent in so doing*** *(ie in selling things). To distinguish this from other money that is spent calls for an understanding of how much things cost*

In communist countries, there used to be no relationship between how much something cost and its price, and shopping was something of a strange experience. It was also a strange experience giving lectures through an interpreter. After saying anything dramatic there is the curious period of delay before reaction shows on the face of the audience (if some of them understand the original English, you then get an echo effect when the translation comes). A colleague was thwarted by the language itself. Attempting to give the famous quote (like many such, ascribed to several different people) that 'the three most important factors in retailing are' – pause for translation into Russian – 'location' – pause – he was surprised when the translation of this one word lasted some fifteen seconds. Suddenly, the prospect of repeating it twice more seemed unwise.

Like Russian, Polish seems to – and does – take longer than English to say the equivalent, but my Polish speaking colleague cleared up a mystery for me at the coffee break in a seminar I was giving. Every time I spoke of 'price and cost', the interpreter would translate what I said and then add words to the effect 'he is saying this is price and that is cost, but we use the words interchangeably in Polish'. I corrected this after the break by stating – for translation – that 'in everyday English, we use the words price and cost interchangeably, but in business they have reserved and different meanings; price is what we charge customers; cost is what we pay for things'. This had quite a dramatic effect on my relationship with the interpreter – but that is another story.

Price and cost

Price certainly is the mechanism by which a business charges its customers, but it is not exactly true that cost is what the business pays for things. In a simple trading business which buys things from one source and sells them on, it is traditional to talk of *cost price* and *selling price* to make the distinction. The use of 'cost price' indicates that something is being paid for. However, if the business makes things itself, or digs material out of the ground, or milks cows, how much do things then cost – and does it matter? The second question is easier to answer than the first, on at least two counts – firstly, the Inland Revenue insists that it matters, and secondly, how can you make a decision about prices if you don't know what your costs are? The first question is harder to answer, because in fact, how much anything costs is qualified by *the set of circumstances surrounding it.*

Actually, businesses such as dairy farming can be ruled out of this discussion, because they do not set prices but take what they are given in the market. This creates an inherent instability which has tended to require government intervention to ensure that, for example, there is an adequate dairy industry. Most of the activities associated with milking have to take place anyway (whatever the price of milk), so while there are probably some relationships between say, winter feed choices and milk yields, costs are not really connected with prices at all.

Expectations of definite relationships between price and cost are the norm in market economies, so that one would not expect to receive in a Western country as I did in Poland a newly-minted 10 zlotysch coin worth one-tenth of a US cent and probably more valuable for its metal content than its exchange value. (There were times when newly minted Italian coinage would disappear immediately, turning up in China for a similar reason.) Even in market systems, not everything has an identifiable cost, nor does every cost count in a decision. The Castner-Kellner process electrolyses concentrated brine to produce sodium hydroxide (its original purpose) and chlorine (its modern application). It is quite impossible to decide how much each chemical costs, because they are created simultaneously.

In the 1970s, the government of a North African State decided (on advice from a firm of international strategy consultants) to raise sharply the price of phosphates, of which their country held much of the world's accessible reserves. The effect of this was overnight to make it economic to mine deposits in Tonga. The Tongans duly started exploiting their reserves, with the effect that where there had previously been a shortage of phosphates, there was now a surplus. The price duly fell (to below its previous level) but this did not put the Tongans off. Having once made the investment, they were wise enough to realise that this was what economists call a sunk cost; not because it was connected with mining, of course, but because closing the mines would not get the investment back. On an operating basis, the Tongan mines were profitable, and they continued to run. It is not recorded whether the consultants received their full fee for the advice.

Economic theory is elegant in its treatment of costs, after the simple assumption that they can actually be measured. Governments insist that they be measured; the Inland Revenue's interest in cost is that it will allow businesses to offset the costs of *what was sold* against revenues for the purpose of calculating liability to taxation, but what was sold and *what was made* can be quite different. To distinguish, a *costing system* is needed.

In the final analysis, someone – frequently an accountant – is charged with the task of counting everything that goes on. This appears to be a sophisticated process, but ultimately it boils down to stating: 'Last year we made 37,965,243 prummets, and we spent £9,827,436 doing it, so the cost of a single prummet is £9,827,436 ÷ 37,965,243 = 25.885 pence'. There are two things to note about this; firstly, it is only true historically – the cost *was* 25.885p. If next year we produce a similar quantity, then the chances are the cost will be similar, but a doubling or halving of prummet production could have all manner of effect on total costs. The second point (rather depending in fact upon what a prummet actually is) is that if it is mass-produced, obtaining just one may not actually be possible, so the idea of the 'unit cost' – so beloved of politicians – is purely notional. The fact that it is quoted to three decimal places does not make it any more real.

Things are usually made in batches (if not in continuous flow), and it is common to divide the costs for the batch by the quantity of items produced, to arrive at an average (or so-called unit) cost. This figure is not meaningful in any other context. A Formula 1 pit team can change four tyres in 8 seconds, but they cannot change one tyre in 2 seconds. Suppose you wanted to make cheese sandwiches. With a large loaf (93p), 200 grams of cheese (97p) and a small tub of margarine (60p), you could produce 10 sandwiches. The total expenditure is £2.50, so each sandwich 'costs' 25 pence. However, you cannot make *one more sandwich* for a further 25p; you would need to buy another loaf of bread. In fact, you would probably have some margarine left from the first batch, say enough for another loaf. This would mean a second batch would 'cost' only 93p + 97p = £1.90, an average of 19 pence. Thinking in terms of the total job, a batch of 20 sandwiches is now said to cost £2.50 + £1.90 = £4.40. The average cost is 22 pence.

Costs then are dependent upon the volume of production (or other activity in the case of intangibles) and thus are liable to vary with changes in volume.

Variations with volume

This concept is also referred to as the *behaviour* of costs – a slightly curious choice of word in its implication that costs somehow 'do it themselves' – but they do follow certain natural principles. We are concerned here with the variations that occur as the *volume of output* changes. Costs also change over time because inputs change with inflation, pay rises, relocation, etc; that is just a further complication for the costing process, and a reason for the existence of such bodies as the Chartered Institute of Management Accountants (originally the less impressively-named Institute of Cost and Works Accountants).

Fixed costs

As the name implies, fixed costs *do not change with volume.* Within reason – that is, for relatively small changes in activity – fixed costs are a constant sum. Examples are rents, business rates, office heating, insurance premiums, the managing director's salary (unless it is performance-related): most things that are generally referred to as overheads. Head office costs and other 'non-productive' aspects of a big business would be regarded as fixed costs, though a distinction would be made for overheads directly incurred at factory level, if they could be regarded as dependent on production. If temporary closure of the factory would save a particular cost, for example power to light the factory, it would be known as a direct overhead. Otherwise, fixed costs are also known as indirect costs.

Variable costs

These are costs which *vary directly with volume* (and are therefore also known as direct costs). The most obvious are costs of goods bought for resale, raw materials bought for manufacture, and the labour and energy used in the process. The important aspect of variation is when change in output produces change in total cost. Costs are not described as variable because, for example, they are a different price every day in the market. The critical question is: if we produce just one more of whatever it is, what will happen to each item in the list of expenditure categories the accountants keep? If it changes, it is a variable cost; if not, it is fixed. This process gives us yet another name, namely *marginal costs* – for costs which vary at the margin of production. Note that it is production, not sales which are relevant. Things produced and not sold are held in stock or inventory where they have some value. (This is one area where service or intangible businesses are easier to cope with. You cannot stockpile haircuts, for example.)

It is obvious that there will be a *range of volumes*, outside which fixed costs will start to change, and average variable costs may be affected. What follows – and indeed, most principles of costing – assume operations within the range. It will generally represent a relatively small percentage compared to the standard, and is thus more appropriate in large, established businesses. Costing in small, dynamic businesses needs to be done carefully.

The basic choice in costing – the process of allocating expenditure to output – is whether fixed costs should be included in the calculation of product costs, or left separate. Neither is entirely satisfactory. For the following calculations, suppose Amalgamated Prummets plc has fixed costs of £10 million, variable costs of £20 million, and produces 10 million prummets annually.

Full, or absorption, costing

As its names imply, this involves allocating the total (*full*) cost of production to the output (which *absorbs* the overhead). The result is:

Total cost (£10m + £20m) = £30m

Total number of prummets = 10 million

Therefore cost per prummet = £3

Strictly speaking, this will hardly ever be true, because the probability is that future production will not be exactly 10 million prummets. If Amalgamated sells its prummets at £5 each, selling exactly 10 million will produce revenues of £50m less costs of £30m, to yield a profit of £20m. This is the same result as the 'unit' calculation, which shows that a profit of £5 – £3 = £2 per prummet, times a volume of 10 million, giving a total profit of £20m.

Using these costings to project different scenarios yields misleading results. Sales of 9 million prummets would indicate a profit on a unit basis of £18m; in fact, the outcome will be: revenue 9 million × £5 = £45m; costs 9 million × £2 (variable) + £10m (fixed) = £28m; therefore profit is £45m – £28m = £17m. Conversely, the forecast for sales of 11 million would indicate a profit of £22m using this system, but the proper calculations from first principles add up to £23m.

The effect of absorption costing is to overstate profit in downturns and understate it in surges. Given that most established business units operating on a large scale will expect to grow by a few per cent annually, the latter is a pleasant bonus, and probably no bad thing psychologically. The former (overstating profit) is quite undesirable, and could be a contributing factor to why managers sometimes fail to anticipate the extent of their losses in periods of severe downturn.

Absorption costing tends to prevail in large scale industry, particularly manufacturing where the allocation process is complicated and there are lots of expenditure categories which are clearly related to the production process even if they are not actually directly variable. Also, the Inland Revenue more or less insists upon it being used.

If the business is very volatile, such as when it is new or growing rapidly, absorption costing can be downright misleading. Rather as a stopped clock is technically correct twice a day whereas one that gains a minute daily is hardly ever exactly right, what matters is which is more helpful for making sensible decisions.

Direct or marginal costing

This method involves specifying costs as a fixed sum plus a unit variable. Costs at Consolidated Prummets (which has identical facilities to Amalgamated) are £10m fixed plus variable of £20m ÷ 10 million prummets = £2 per prummet. This method of presentation means that cost forecasts for different volumes will now be accurate, but it still begs the question of what volume will be sold – and what the price should therefore be to ensure that fixed costs are covered and a profit is generated. Manufactured prices are often decided by adding a percentage to average cost. In the absorption costing example, it was two-thirds or 67% (£3 + £2 = £5); applying the same amount to the direct costing example gives a price of £2 × 1.67 = £3.34, and a profit per unit of £1.34. Volume changes do not under- or overstate this profit – within the range of relevant volumes, it is correct. Sales of 10 million prummets result in a *gross profit* (also known as *contribution*) of £13.4m, out of which the fixed costs of £10m have to be met. The net profit is only £3.4m. Clearly, it is important to understand which costing system is being used, if it is also to be used to determine prices by adding a percentage mark-up.

To achieve a profit of £10m at a price of £3.34 would obviously require an increase in sales. The situation is that at a level of 10 million prummets, fixed costs have been met, and there is a net profit of £3.4m. A further £6.6m contribution is sought, which is generated at the rate of £1.34 per prummet. Additional sales of £6.6m ÷ £1.34 = 4.9 million prummets are needed.

It is unlikely that such an increase in sales of nearly 50 per cent could be achieved without affecting other costs, so, to repeat the message, this method is also limited by the scope or range of variation on output over which it applies. Subject to this limitation, the direct costing method provides possibly the single most valuable tool in the management handbook.

Breakeven

This is a simple algebraic device (for those people who freeze at the mention of algebra it can also be done graphically, see The

The Breakeven Chart

The horizontal axis indicates the volume of sales by physical measure, and the vertical axis the money involved.

The revenue line passes through the origin O, since zero sales produces zero revenue, and is a straight line because price is constant.

The total cost line passes through point F, since at zero sales the fixed costs are incurred. To this value F is added the variable costs which also increase in line with volume.

Because variable costs per unit are less than the price, the total cost line slopes less than the revenue line. Where the two lines intersect is the breakeven point, when revenue equals total cost. The volume and revenue can be read off from the axes, and the profit or loss for a given volume either side of the breakeven position is the difference between the values shown on the price and cost lines.

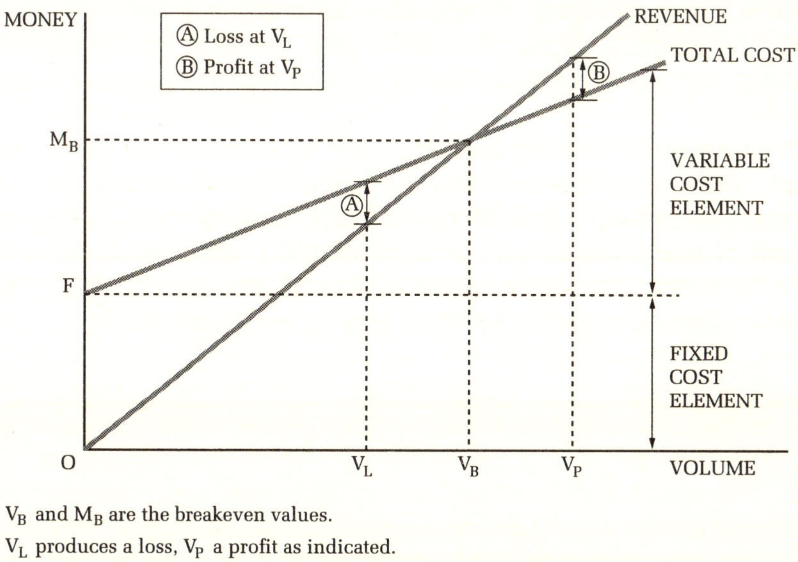

V_B and M_B are the breakeven values.

V_L produces a loss, V_P a profit as indicated.

Breakeven Chart) which aims to use fixed and variable costs to calculate volumes and prices which will yield a profit of exactly zero – that is, to find the level at which the business will break even. This is called – unsurprisingly – the breakeven point. The calculation for Amalgamated Prummets is straightforward – contribution per unit is £3 (price £5 less variable cost of £2), the fixed costs are £10m, so the volume at which it will make exactly zero profit (also neither a profit nor a loss, just cover its total costs, break even) is 10,000,000 ÷ 3 = 3,333,333 prummets.

Clearly the prummet business is readily profitable (perhaps Amalgamated has a patent to limit competition). In more competitive industries, you might find figures such as these for United Fossets Inc: fossets sell for $3, and have a variable cost of $2.25; a proposed new facility can turn out up to 50 million per year, with fixed costs of $36 million, for an investment of $40 million. Should it be built? Let's see:

The contribution per fosset sold is $3 – $2.25 = $0.75
Fixed costs are $36m
The number of fossets to cover fixed costs is therefore
$36m ÷ $0.75 = 48 million

This figure is very close to capacity (96%, ie 48 out of an available 50 million) and the project looks unlikely to be viable. Using the figures another way, assuming the plant can work at 100%, the contribution is $0.75 × 50 million = $37.5m. Fixed costs are $36m, so the maximum net profit is $1.5m, a poor return on an investment of $40m.

The choices for United are to go back to the drawing board and:

(a) design a plant with lower fixed costs, *or*
(b) build a plant with a bigger capacity (without a commensurate increase in fixed costs), *or*
(c) design a method of reducing variable costs, *or*
(d) give up

Suppose United now plans a fosset plant with a capacity of 100 million a year, fixed costs of $60 million and a slight reduction in variable costs to $2.20 per fosset. The investment is $70m.

Contribution is now $0.80 per fosset, so breakeven occurs at

\$60m ÷ \$0.80 = 75 million units, or 75% of capacity. The upside profit potential at capacity is 25 million × \$0.80 = \$20m net profit, so the investment looks more promising.

These are the famous back-of-the-envelope calculations[1] traditionally said to have been the origin of nearly every business. For a situation like that at United Fossets, the decisions often hinge around finding an optimum size of plant, but the result may add a significant chunk to world capacity, a factor which may have an affect on prices (as with the phosphate mines). If United decide that an extra 100 million a year on world fosset production will result in a price decline of 10% (that is, from \$3 to \$2.70), contribution declines to \$0.50 per unit and the new plant cannot break even. How such investment decisions are eventually made is clearly another story.

In the case of a very small business, the capacity choice may have little impact on the world (and the 'going rate' may be taken as read for the price), but what is required is a more thorough consideration of how costs will vary. The important thing to remember about breakeven is that it only applies to a certain range of volumes, essentially those for which 'fixed costs' actually stay fixed.

There are business options which try to ensure that costs are as variable, or as fixed as they can be. The former involves using subcontractors to undertake manufacturing, whose supplies will be charged pretty much at a set rate per unit. This has the advantage – provided other things such as availability and lead times are equal – of ensuring a definite cost in unpredictable circumstances where volume needs might go outside the relevant range, thus rendering in-house manufactured costs volatile. The disadvantage is that no scale advantages accrue as volumes increase. The alternative of mostly fixed costs is found in production flow lines such as for cars. Material and component costs obviously remain variable, but all others are essentially fixed. Provided high capacity utilisation is maintained, costs per car are the lowest achievable. Problems with this scenario arise when there are volume reductions which cannot be matched by

---

[1] In the days when smoking was the norm, people would refer to 'the back of a fag packet' in this context. If the Swedish Post Office is correct – and it has given everyone over the age of eight an e-mail address – envelopes are set to become something of a rarity. What will we use then?

reduced costs on the production line, resulting in a higher cost per car.

Cost behaviour revisited

It may have already occurred to you that in real life, most costs are neither exactly fixed, nor exactly variable. Some costs are genuinely fixed (by legal agreement in the case of commercial rents) but most increase as so-called step functions (named from their appearance in a chart). Increases in volume are accommodated until such a time as a new 'lump' is needed. Wages of people involved in production are treated as variable costs by necessity, and if pay is strictly for piece work, this is so. However, workers may expect minimum wages irrespective of output levels, so there is a possible fixed element.

Many overheads are semi-fixed (or semi-variable, depending on one's point of view). You would expect the consumption of stationery, electricity, telephone calls, and photocopying etc to increase if you double the staff in a small office, but you would not expect them to double, whereas they would if you opened another office. Some costs may actually decline with volume increases: for example, a firm may decide it no longer needs the same level of advertising, once it has built a client base or reputation. Others are at management's discretion, not automatically incurred, but subject to decisions. Advertising in media like Yellow Pages would fall into this category, where the decision on expenditure would have to be taken in anticipation. The ultimate residual cost (incurred only after everything else is settled) of a very small business is likely to be the proprietor's salary. For this reason – and even if the proprietor does not realise it – the question 'What is your breakeven point?' to a self-employed person is seriously impertinent.

WHERE TO NEXT?

Cost allocation is an issue in the selling process (Chapter 4)
Also an important element in the marketing mix (Chapter 10)
A large element of fixed costs is actually depreciation (Chapter 13)
Controlling costs is a necessary – but not sufficient – condition for success (Chapter 20)

8. Service and service businesses

*When the things to be **sold repeatedly over time** are intangible, questions of perceived benefits and good value assume prominence*

There are undoubtedly many respects in which services are different from products. You can store a product, modify it after it is made, or gift-wrap it, none of which you can obviously do with a service. From a business perspective, if you fail to sell a product today, you can recover by selling it tomorrow, but you cannot recover the wasted time if you fail to sell a service. In either case though, you need a customer.

A Chinese proverb states, 'If a man is hungry, I don't give him a fish, I teach him how to fish.' This embodies the admirable principle that assistance should be enabling and not denigrating, but the maxim has limitations. The man may learn a technique that works during a certain season, and then starve when the fish move to other waters. The really effective approach is to teach him to understand – and be able to predict – the behaviour of fish. So it is with business; for fish, read customers. If you want to understand how service businesses work, begin with a study of the behaviour of customers. Like the fisherman, the service business is seeking to attract and hook its prey, but it does not seek to devour it, hoping instead to establish a mutually beneficial trading relationship. Unfortunately, the behaviour of customers is more complex than that of fish!

Benefits and needs

Products may possess features of direct and indirect relationship to their functions, some of which manufacturers introduce not because they are essential, but to make their products more 'attractive' than competitors'. Customers do not buy the *features*; they need to obtain *benefits* from them, and for that to happen, customers must have – or someone must create within them – *needs* which the product can satisfy.

There are two important aspects of the concept of needs. Firstly, almost everything that we now find indispensable in modern life once upon a time did not exist, so it follows that needs are acquired. Secondly, it is fundamental to human behaviour to satisfy needs when they arise, and if this cannot be done, then to rationalise away their existence. Thus it is rare for sales representatives to find large numbers of people just waiting to have their needs satisfied with the products they are toting. Hence, much effort in sales training courses and manuals goes into identifying – and if necessary, creating – needs. Eventually, there then follows a general conversion process (with which we are familiar) when what was once considered an expensive luxury becomes an affordable necessity – but necessity is usually the child, not the mother, of invention.

The issue of whether there are fundamental differences between products and services is complex. The argument exists that since it is the benefits of any purchase which consumers ultimately appreciate, then there is no real difference. Benefits are ultimately intangible, being psychological in nature (in all non-essential circumstances). On the other hand, it is obvious that it is possible to sample or try products (clothes, for example) in a way that it is not for services (for instance haircuts). Also, services are not usually transferable (you cannot give someone else the haircut you have just paid for) nor are they storable. A major issue in service businesses is that commonly benefits can only be appreciated *after* the customer has agreed to purchase, and consumed the item in question. This normally requires the customer to assess the salience of the benefits offered in advance – to estimate how much better off he or she will feel against the price being asked, a difficult task if there is no prior experience of the specific service.

Purchasing behaviour

There are recorded circumstances of prices being left to the customer's discretion after the consumption, but they are rare. Fads for pay-what-it's-worth restaurants have not lasted long for example, though in certain cultures the general phenomenon is more common. Chinese people pay their acupuncturist when they are well, a concept which actually makes considerable sense, but is not exactly consistent with Western approaches to health care. (It used to be the case before the NHS that GPs would charge patients according to their ability to pay, and this was generally accepted by patients as being 'fair' – though in truth, there was often no alternative doctor available anyway.) Devotees of religious sects are often expected to contribute according to their means, but those organised religions which are the most economically sound are also those which tend to specify the proportion of income which should be contributed.

Of course, there are times when people will make purchasing decisions without considering the price, notably in emergencies and crises. Mostly, though, people try to assess the quality of the service offered to see if it appears worth the price. As with products, there are big differences between frequent and infrequent purchases. There are businesses classified as services such as restaurants where there is some frequency of purchase, some shopping around, and where consumers are generally familiar with what is on offer – and have realistic expectations. Whether these are genuinely service businesses or 'seriously enhanced products' is open to debate.

Pure intangibles where the customer is venturing into the unknown are different. The man whose psychotherapist fell asleep during an account of a particularly painful episode in his life ought in retrospect to have walked out of the consultation, but the relationship between client and therapist is such that the client probably thought it was his own fault. Intangibles often do not – or should not – entail repeat purchasing – no one should need more than one vasectomy, for example – but where they form part of regular consumption patterns people do not as a rule shop around. Although there may be occasional change from time to time, people tend to have only one dentist, one accountant, etc at a time. This may be because it is not possible to sample different ones in action. Two dentists working on the same toothache is not practical, and the idea of asking several accountants to compile and submit tax returns so that you can choose the one who obtains the lowest tax liability is intriguing, but not realistic. If you only have one, it can be hard to judge if you are getting value for money from your accountant, or dentist, or psychotherapist.

Value for money

This is actually a very odd expression; does it imply that people frequently spend money on things that do not have value? *Collins Dictionary*, 1987 edition, lists it as a term for satisfaction, but I could not locate a reference in the OED (second edition). Whatever value for money (VFM) may mean linguistically, it describes a concept central to consumer buying experience. It implies the existence of a kind of personal reference system, by which any 'offer of supply' can be assessed, both in expectation and perception, before purchase, and again during or after consumption. Although consumers do not necessarily keep files, or even 'make mental notes', they accumulate experience and refine their concepts of VFM in different situations. There are a number of points to note:

- It is a relative measure. The perceived VFM of any single offer is a function of the alternatives that exist at the time.

- It is a personal judgment. What one person considers good VFM, another may consider an extravagance or substandard. Much depends upon the appeal to the individual of the underlying benefits to be obtained from the purchase.

- Perceptions of value vary according to circumstances for an individual. Most people are prepared to spend more on a meal eaten out (and consider it good value) than they are on a meal for the home, for example.

Price, delivery and quality (PDQ)

Anyone supplying a service would prefer it to be unique and therefore not subject to comparisons, but most of the time genuine differentiation is not achievable. Service suppliers are left to compete on a VFM basis through the strategy of combining the three dimensions of Price, Delivery and Quality, in a configuration different from competitors. Offers which are markedly good in the consumer's perception on one of these dimensions are poor in the others. Typically, suppliers offer a 'good' combination along two dimensions, remaining less competitive in the third. Consumers are so familiar with this situation as to expect it implicitly. Hence, when it is suddenly changes – in a severe shortage, or a January Sale, for example – consumer behaviour changes sharply.

Price in this context refers to the monetary exchange which will take place, and may be influenced – it certainly will be in organisational markets – by credit terms and limits, settlement discounts, etc. *Delivery* refers to all temporal aspects of the purchase from the buyer's perspective, and includes factors such as availability, convenience, waiting times, etc; and *Quality* covers all performance-related attributes of what is being purchased, both tangible and cosmetic, real and perceived. Because of the nature of competition, there are very few examples to be cited of a business being superior to its competitors on all three of these dimensions. Either it is unprofitable (which is how some new businesses start out) or its suppliers' prices are being squeezed.

The particular combination of PDQ sought by the customer can change according to circumstances, most obviously when time is of the essence, and delivery factors dominate. The consumer with a sudden change of circumstances might naturally expect to use a different supplier. A supplier who builds a certain reputation cannot easily change it and retain the same customer base.

This is apparent with immature business propositions, such as the recently-opened popular restaurant providing excellent meals at cheap prices. As word spreads, to avoid having queues, it must become fast-food-chain-like in its approach to serving customers, or set up a reservation system, or increase the prices. All three of these changes will result in a change of clientele. (You may like to consider the choices from which you select when you are about to purchase services – the PDQ factors are most likely to be present in every case. With the 'enhanced benefit' view of products as services, PDQ factors influence just about every buying decision.)

In the discussion of the marketing strategies of plumbers on page 107, PDQ factors appear by name. The emergency plumber competes by being able to deliver very quickly – the price is high and the quality adequate for the purpose. The domestic plumber competes on a quality-price combination, and customers are prepared to wait until the person they have chosen can schedule the job. The subcontract buyer demands a certain price, but delivery is also critical otherwise overall progress (and project costs) are affected. You can form your own conclusions about the quality of plumbing in new housing developments.

In general terms, PDQ combinations correspond in manufacturing to the E-strategies described in Chapter 6. Efficiency means providing quality at a low cost, and hence price. It may involve a wait. Viewing P, D, and Q as the corners of a triangle, *efficiency* lies on the PQ side, and is weak on D. *Effectiveness* costs more to provide, and must charge more, so it is based on the DQ side, being weak on P. On the third, PD, side of the triangle is *economy*, and Q is poor.

As mentioned, PDQ is implicit in everyday choice. What follows may not quite apply to your personal preferences, but suppose you fancy eating fish and chips this evening. You have the choice of a takeaway from a Fish & Chip Shop, going to a Fish Restaurant, or Cooking Your Own. Other things being equal:[1]

In terms of *price*, the attractiveness should be:

1st Cook Your Own **2nd** Fish & Chip Shop **3rd** Restaurant

(This assumes you have the facilities to cook etc; your fish may not be much cheaper than the shop, but your chips will be.)

From a *delivery* perspective, cooking is the slowest (you have to go out first and buy the fish). The order of attractiveness is now:

1st Fish & Chip Shop **2nd** Restaurant **3rd** Cook Your Own

Quality is more subjective, and – with apologies to some of the Great British Fish & Chip Shops – the ranking ought to be:

1st Restaurant **2nd** Cook Your Own **3rd** Fish & Chip Shop

Perhaps not everyone agrees with these rankings, but for most people, each option scores a first, a second, and a third.

---

[1] This is a favoured term of economists, who often use the Latin *ceteris paribus*. In real life, it is remarkably difficult to tell whether other things are in fact equal.

Marketing services to organisations

In the marketing of services, PDQ is a helpful way of understanding competitive situations, and there are different implications for the initial recruitment and subsequent retention of customers. Organisational markets are characterised by a tendency for supplier-customer relationships to emerge in preference to a reliance on 'shopping around'. Thus, competing suppliers of products have difficulty opening new accounts, but at least they should be able to present, discuss and compare their products from time to time.

The suppliers of 'pure' services face the added complication that the potential customer's experience is intangible and not transferable. Moreover, the buyer placing the order may not be the actual consumer. The seller cannot easily offer the 'prospect' an opportunity to compare the experience, since this would require the latter to commit to a purchase (or it would have to be provided free of charge). Patently, unless the buyer is actually strongly dissatisfied with the existing supplier, there is no reason to do this. The buyer will maintain, reasonably, that the acceptable quality of a known supplier is better than the putative improvements of an unknown (for who will be to blame within the organisation if there is a switch of suppliers which misfires?).

The seller may offer a reduced price as an introductory offer, but in most circumstances, this is not wise; if the buyer accepts the offer, quality cannot actually be paramount. It must be a lesser factor, with the opportunity to save money having greater importance, at least to the individual making the decision. Thus, even if the new supplier then demonstrates improvements in quality, how much will these be deemed to be worth in the eyes of the buyer, when there was nothing actually wrong with the original? The probability is that if the order is repeated, the buyer will expect and require the reduced price again, which is not what the seller has in mind.

Arguably, it would be better to offer the buyer a free version instead of a reduced price, since this is setting no precedents for what future prices might be. This tactic is not guaranteed to be successful either, because it can be very difficult to assess the value of something when it is actually provided free!

Consequently, the most likely way a service business acquires new customers who already buy similar services elsewhere is through its capacity to deliver. When the regular supplier is unable to deliver and the service must be provided, then the quality risk is worth taking. This is in contrast to the dimensions which retain customers, where the Q-P relationship in PDQ is dominant.

Of course, this is a simplistic view of what in practice can be a complex set of variables and relationships. Much depends upon the experience of the parties involved. When an organisation is buying for the first time, its perceptions of quality – and thence value – will be rather unreliable. If the supplier is offering a newly introduced service with which the buyer is already familiar, then it is probably necessary for the supplier to trade on the buyer's terms. When neither has done it before, anything may happen. The construction of Eurotunnel was a unique service; was it also good value for money?

Tendering

Firms that compete for contracts through competitive tendering live with PDQ factors permanently. They exist side by side because when one firm wins a contract (or accumulates a number of small orders) it is taken out of the frame for future bids. Each firm must be essentially capable, and it is assumed that it does not bid for contracts unless it is technically able to fulfil them. A competitor with a new contract is disadvantaged in bidding for the next; either it bids a later completion date, or a higher price (reflecting increased costs of working overtime, hiring new staff, subcontracting etc). Failing this, it puts in a 'silly bid' – one which it cannot deliver and which will damage its reputation if it is accepted. People awarding the contract choose another firm because they are sufficiently well informed to spot the silly bid. Another firm joins the list of non-contenders for the next contract and so the work is shared out. The idea that competitive tendering is the most objective form of purchasing is not true for this reason; it depends upon the subjective assessment by the client of the bidder's ability to deliver the specified quality at the quoted price. If it did not, silly bids would be accepted and contracts would continually foul up. This sometimes happens in periods of severe recession, when large contractors try and hang on to their resources by taking on loss-making contracts, but most of the time, it does not.

Such competitive environments depend for their stability upon the circulation of public knowledge, so where a firm has a genuine advantage, it needs somehow to keep it to itself, if the supplier, and not the customer, is to benefit.

Suppose that in the prummet industry there are lots of similar firms who provide subcontract cordwangling, but one, Rumpo Cordwangling Ltd, has a genuine advantage. Where other firms take 100 hours to cordwangle a gross of prummets, Rumpo takes only 80. Throughout the industry, there will be an expected charge rate on which contracts are priced, say £10 per hour. If Rumpo uses this rate, when tendering for a contract for cordwangling 5 gross prummets, it will pass on its advantage as follows:

Any Old Cordwangler Ltd – Quotation

5 gross prummets cordwangled @ 100 hours per gross
Total job 5 × 100 = 500 hours
Price 500 hours @ £10 = £5000

Rumpo Cordwangling Ltd – Quotation 1

5 gross prummets cordwangled @ 80 hours per gross
Total job 5 × 80 = 400 hours
Price 400 hours @ £10 = £4000

So, the customer gains £1000.

Because of its advantage, Rumpo can charge a premium, say £12 per hour, and still be competitive:

Rumpo Cordwangling Ltd – Quotation 2

5 gross prummets cordwangled @ 80 hours per gross
Total job 5 × 80 = 400 hours
Price 400 hours @ £12 = £4800

The buyer should not accept this quote, as the rate is too high. Rumpo should only be used in an emergency when a premium price can be justified. (This is not an entirely logical conclusion, but it is a natural one). Hence, to get the contract the quote should be presented as:

Rumpo Cordwangling Ltd – Quotation 3

5 gross prummets cordwangled @ 96 hours per gross
Total job 5 × 96 = 480 hours
Price 480 hours @ £10 = £4800

This way, Rumpo will finish the job quicker than its customer expects. Hence, it can also deliver before the quoted completion date, and thus add a little 'extra value' for its customer, while keeping the lion's share for itself.

If you did not believe it before, I hope you now accept the assertion that when a firm offers higher quality, faster, at a lower price than its competitors, it is subsidising its customers. If it manages to make a profit while it does so, it must be obtaining a similar subsidy from its suppliers.

WHERE TO NEXT?

Advertising can reinforce the service experience (Chapter 2)
Strategies for entering markets and maintaining position can differ (Chapter 12)
Trading relationships need to show profits (Chapter 16)
Service extends throughout an organisation (Chapter 20)

Section 3

Facing the wider environment

9. Loyalty and loss leaders

Purchases made repeatedly, over time, give consumers vast experience which manufacturers and retailers should respect

Nineteen ninety-six was the year of the loyalty card. All sorts of retailers joined the rush to introduce smart cards on which their customers could record 'points' when they shopped. It was also the year that Lord MacLaurin was appointed head of the England and Wales Cricket Board, in recognition of the fact that cricket was not 'just a game' but a self-funding branch of the entertainment industry, which needed to be more business-like in its approach. Lord MacLaurin had risen to the top of the tree at Tesco, which had recently taken over from Sainsburys as the United Kingdom's largest retailer by revenue. As Ian MacLaurin, one of his first contributions in the Tesco boardroom – boldly, in the presence of the founder, Lord Cohen – was to propose discontinuing Green Shield Stamps, in favour of plain low prices. Green Shield were the leading brand of so-called trading stamps, issued to customers in proportion to the amount of money spent. They could be collected, stuck into special books, and eventually redeemed for goods available from a catalogue. Retailers bought the stamps from the company, but of course, not all customers got round to cashing them in. The major beneficiary of the scheme appeared to be the Green Shield Stamp company; at least, its managing director enjoyed for a time the reputation of being the highest paid executive in Britain.

Loyalty schemes

Trading stamps were a reward scheme, but not exactly loyalty-based as they were available in many places, including petrol stations and, on one particular day as a promotion, inside every copy of the *Daily Express*. MacLaurin's decision was that they were not doing Tesco any good. It was American Airlines who first realised that, as all their ticketing systems were computerised, it was actually possible to find out who – by name – was actually flying with them. To their surprise, the data revealed that as many as 50 per cent of all flights were undertaken by only 4 per cent of their customers. In other words, there was a core of frequent flyers who spent serious amounts of money with airlines. These were desirable customers, and American Airlines introduced the world's first frequent flyer programme. This did not involve sticking stamps into books, as by now the smart card had been invented. For a short while, the programme may have been said to work, although it must have been hard to tell in reality. American Advantage customers (as they were known) certainly had their needs anticipated by airline staff each time they flew, and perhaps other incentives – expressed in the form of free flights for relatives, etc – would encourage people to try American first. However, in terms of business travel within the USA (which is the category most people fell into) the overwhelmingly important factor in the choice of carrier would be the timing of the flight in relation to the person's own schedule. Furthermore, the person's flight would probably be booked by someone else, an assistant, or secretary who would not obviously benefit from the scheme.

Thus, the reward for being 'loyal' to American Airlines was in most cases no more than a bonus for using common sense, though it may have made a slight difference at the margin (and we would need privileged information to judge this by). It certainly made a difference to the airline industry; the thing about something like a frequent flyer programme is that you cannot prevent other airlines from adopting the same idea, so before long, more or less every airline had one. Each feels it must, by which time, it is no more than a form of taxation, as every airline now has to give away free seats for the passengers it would have obtained anyway. An added complication is a reciprocal scheme, which removes the need for loyalty. Of course, the scheme might be a good one, if people went out of their way to collect miles and then forgot to use them – but can anyone seriously be expected to do this on a consistent basis?

The MacLaurin-inspired move to low prices at Tesco occasionally led them into 'price wars' – the effects of which through periods of high inflation were difficult to chart precisely – and around the end of the 1970s, it appeared that they 'scared' themselves with over-enthusiastic discounting. They decided henceforth to compete on the quality of their merchandise. This was good news for Sainsbury's who were able to continue with their own approach to quality, and for many other supermarket operators who were able to compete underneath Sainsbury's price 'umbrella'. The slogan 'Good food costs less at Sainsbury's' – which has been around for over twenty years – does not actually specify what it costs less than! Tesco's reformation took a long time, for it is all very well to run a new advertising campaign, and start buying superior merchandise, but if your stores are located in areas which are convenient to people who are used to, and *like*, seeing you 'pile it high and sell it cheap', the conversion is heavy going. Essentially, Tesco only finally achieved its objectives by relocating its stores, at the same time increasing store size – which was also a part of the strategy – and it took about a decade.

Consumer behaviour

Visits to supermarkets, and purchases of the things they sell, are by and large frequent events. They account for massive amounts of money, and some has been put back into finding out how the purchasing patterns of individuals or family units vary over time. Information about specific brands has been useful to the manufacturers and to stores; aggregate information about the market shares of different brands – and how individuals contribute to the overall effect – has interested academic researchers. The usual method of data collection has been through consumer panels, people who record their purchases systematically. Subject to the proviso that there is something inherently strange about anyone who participates in such a panel – and much effort has gone into controlling for such bias – the same patterns of results have occurred over the last fifty years, in Europe, the USA and Japan, for different demographic subgroups, over periods ranging from one week to one year, for a very wide range of products.[1]

The conclusion is that people are not loyal; they have preferences, but the number that buy only one brand of a class

[1] For a list of products for which these findings hold, see for example *Repeat Buying* by A.S.C. Ehrenberg, Griffin, 1988.

of product is very few. It varies slightly with the type of product, but roughly, in one week 70%, in three months 30%, and in one year, only about 10% of people who bought a given brand bought no others.

This is disappointing news to brand managers, and to consumers. Generally, people don't like these findings on first hearing them. They like to think of themselves as efficient, loyal, intelligent shopping machines. Some people can get quite upset when it is suggested that they are not loyal shoppers (and experience suggests it is best to leave them with their beliefs), but the occurrence is not particularly common. When asked, most people think back and recognise a description of their own behaviour, and an overall picture is created dramatically when they are asked to consider the behaviour of six people they know well who have otherwise as little as possible in common.

A commonsense explanation of shopping patterns which has merit is that it is more or less impossible to be efficient, loyal, and intelligent every time, all the time. It is not efficient to travel miles to another shop if your local shops are out of your favourite brand of biscuits, and it is not intelligent to refuse to sample other brands to compare with your preference. It is intelligent to visit all your supermarkets to check on relative prices, but not efficient if you are also working and providing for a home and family. It may be efficient to buy potatoes by the 25kg sack, but not intelligent if you are travelling by bicycle.

The importance of things being frequently purchased is that there is feedback from the experience which has a bearing on the next event. This is not the case with infrequent purchases (of which by far the worst-prepared decision for many people is a home, but that is another story). Broadly under discussion here are what is commonly referred to as FMCGs – fast moving consumer goods. (Just in case there is doubt, a Ferrari is not an FMCG – the F refers to how long the things take to be sold.) There are two dimensions to consumer behaviour, technically known as the cognitive and the affective. People have knowledge about what they consume, and they also have feelings. A brand can therefore mean several things, as outlined in Chapter 2. At the cognitive level, the brand is a shorthand form of identity which describes the quality of the product. Affectively, it may also make the purchaser feel proud to be consuming it. The emotional aspects are just as valid as the functional, and the use of the word 'loyalty' implies both a fact and a commitment.

The scientific interpretation of an individual purchasing occasion is to deem it *as if stochastic*. A stochastic event is one which occurs as a result of random influences from a large number of variables. With a purchase, the influences may not be random, but they are sufficiently varied as to be effectively unpredictable in any given circumstance. A consumer may have definite intentions, but be unable to execute them. The same pattern of (non-loyal) behaviour for products has been observed for stores – one obvious explanation of why people may not always buy the same brand if they are not offered the same choice in different stores.[2]

If a particular brand is a leader in its field (that is, it has the biggest share of sales) it is not because of loyal consumers; it is because, of all those people buying the product class, more buy the brand leader during a given time period; and of all those buying the brand leader, they choose that brand more often than others. The converse of this is for a small brand, which is bought by few people, infrequently. Big brands have more than proportionate advantages over small ones in terms of promotional spend, based on the ease with which the audience can be reached.

The exception to this observation is where a market is segmented. Segmentation occurs where there is sufficient distinction between what appear to be similar products for them not to be substitutable. Indeed, conditions in which these usual results break down could be put forward as a proper definition for a segmented market. All brand managers dream of creating segmentation in their own market areas, but the consumer knows best. Through frequent purchasing – at relatively low-risk expenditure levels – consumers compare, contrast, and remember. The consumer is sovereign, in effect.

Despite all this evidence, it still seems as though brand managers believe in brand loyalty, and use it as a model for designing promotions which are destined to be unsuccessful before they start. The basic idea is to provide some kind of incentive to sample their brand, whereupon people will like it

---

[2] The advent of store loyalty schemes means that it will at last be possible in complete confidentiality to examine individual purchasing patterns over time using electronic checkout data, removing the need for other incentives which maintain people's membership of consumer panels. It will not record their purchases in other stores, of course.

so much, they will change their habits. By definition, this incentive cannot be a feature of the experience of the consumption of the brand, so it must involve some kind of unrelated benefit which encourages someone to switch from their usual brand, to which they are therefore showing scant loyalty. (Note that the evidence does not state that people do not have a 'usual brand', only that they do not buy it exclusively.)

Meanwhile, the stores through which this brand is sold may appear to believe in the concept of the 'loss leader' – the proposition being that consumers will visit the store because something is on sale very cheap, and while they are there, make all their other purchases because it is convenient, without counting the cost. Despite an obvious flaw – the assumption that people are not merely occasionally, but persistently, stupid – the loss leader has found its way into popular awareness in the manner of few other concepts from business. However, the incontrovertible fact is, changing the price of something changes the consumer's perception of it, and hence their behaviour towards it.

Re-launches

A past Chief Executive of a well-known Anglo Dutch consumer goods company is reported to have been asked at a conference:

'Do you believe in re-launches (of dying brands)?' To which he replied:

'Not really.'

'Why not?'

'Well, they don't work.'

'Why then does your company do them?'

'The marketing department has to have something to do.'

This is one of those good stories which the truth might spoil, but does it imply that there are times when a marketing department is needed – such as to launch a new product – and the rest of the time, it should twiddle its thumbs? It is true that most re-launches do not succeed, and that something like four out of five[3] new products fail. Nevertheless, is it the marketing

---

[3] There are various statistics quoted for the failure of new products, depending on different definitions of the starting points, such as concept, prototype, consumer trial, test market etc. They all show that only a small minority succeed.

department's job to accept these statistics – effectively conceding defeat before it starts – or should it set out to beat the odds? If it is going to receive the same budget allocation in either case, the vote should surely go to the latter, even if the circumstances which bring success are not always within the department's control.

One famous example in Britain (which wasn't a launch, just a new promotion) involved the long-running advertising campaign featuring the theme 'Heineken refreshes the parts . . .' In anticipation of a successful campaign (that is, in the belief that they would beat the odds) the brewers laid in extra stocks; what they did not anticipate was that the country would experience a drought. The concept of drinking chilled, canned lager beers was relatively new at the time, and the young trend-setting population were encouraged by the conditions to take up the habit. As other brewers ran out of stocks, Heineken was there to refresh the refrigerators other lagers could not reach, and meanwhile, the advertising agency ran a series of literally up-to-the minute press adverts mimicking efforts to bring the drought to an end. The brand experienced a significant leap in market share which lasted many years.

On a possibly healthier note, a famous re-launch which beat the odds was that of Lucozade. This glucose-based 'health drink' had carved itself such a reputation in the 1950s – without the help of TV advertising and supermarkets, whose influence was yet to be felt – that it became a drink *kids could only have if they were ill.* It was so 'precious' that the family-sized bottle was wrapped in tinted cellophane, so, while it commanded a premium price, there was a serious limit to its penetration (how many households bought it) and its frequency (how often they did).

As what we might call the modern marketing mix evolved – TV advertising, supermarkets, creative and disposable packaging, set in a youth culture – so Lucozade suffered the 'double jeopardy' of being a small brand, with few people buying it, infrequently. (It may have been that every sick child wanted Lucozade, but by no means every parent felt they could afford it.) In the 1980s, it was resuscitated in remarkable style. Handily re-packaged for on-the-move, fitness-conscious young people, available through convenience stores, Lucozade was introduced in adverts featuring people such as Daley Thompson, Olympic and World Decathlon Champion, and England and Liverpool footballer John Barnes, as 'the energy drink' for a new generation. The product range was extended by alternative flavourings, and it included an isotonic 'Sport' version, for really fast fluid replacement. In all probability, the isotonic effect was achieved through a more dilute version of the drink, but of course, it could command a premium price. This was possibly brilliant marketing.

What is probably the best known brand in the world – Coca-Cola – is a soft drink, and while the name has never been extended to other products, there is its companion brand Diet Coke. Whether this serves as a beacon to all people in the drinks industry – 'we must have a diet version' – or whether the passage of time and changes in staff mean that original premises on which a product is based are overlooked, or whether comments like the Chief Executive's about marketing departments are in fact accurate – for whatever reason, there is now a low calorie version of Lucozade. This is worth repeating – *a low calorie version of The Energy Drink*! A calorie is, of course, a measure of the energy stored in a food.

Brand management

Launching new (or revitalised) products may be the exceptional part of a brand manager's work, for the real stock-in-trade is attempting to boost sales of existing brands. In fact, this statement should read 'boost profit contribution' according to the theories, but as mentioned elsewhere, sales volumes are easier to measure than profits, and market share is a nice competitive concept. There are in fact only three objectives the brand manager can have, namely

- to increase the size of the purchase (make me buy more)
- to increase the frequency (make me buy more often)
- to increase the penetration (make me buy when ordinarily I would not), which can be split into: more trials, and more switches. Trials are of product categories I do not normally buy; switches are changes of brands.

Any particular promotion may involve a combination of the three.

In the interests of making a scientific observation, I took a stroll round a nearby supermarket to see what kind of offerings brand managers were making in the spring of 1997. There are a couple of important things to note about my expedition: firstly, I am expressing my own reactions, to which I am quite entitled, and I am not supposing that any particular person might behave in any particular way. (I mention this because there are people who believe it is politically incorrect to attribute behavioural patterns to social groups.) Secondly, my conclusions are in two senses invalid. The only arbiter of success is the sales figures (or profit) that are attributable to the exercise – it is the aggregate effect across all consumers that counts. Also, as I did not buy the things I noticed, I cannot suppose that I would react the same way if I had actually been shopping. Finally, it is not always clear whether a promotion is the work of the manufacturer, the store, or a combination of both. The flexibility provided by bar coding makes the difference difficult to discern; specially printed packets might suggest the manufacturer is the source, but with the largest retailers, even these can be specially prepared.

The first thing I noticed was just how many promotions there were. As stated, I cannot speak for anyone else, but following a shopping list usually restricts my own view to those items on it. Also, three members of the public, seeing me with a notebook in hand, asked for advice, and although no member of staff challenged me, I do not think I will do this again. In no particular order, I selected:

- Frozen Oriental Express Veg Mix, normally £1.45, now 99p until the end of the month
- Mini Muesli (single serving) 23p
- Persil, 3kg £4.69, with Free Comfort (2 litres) worth £1.79
- The Store's Honey 89p for 227 grams, but only £1.35 for 454 grams
- Ready-to-Eat Jelly, down from 35p to 25p
- Finish Dishwasher powder 1kg £2.99, get 800g of the same free, worth £2.29
- Variety pack cereals, normally 6 packs, now 8 including two packs free
- Gordon's Gin, buy 2 bottles, £1 off each
- Luxury Quilted Toilet Tissue, nine roll pack – buy 1 get a second half price while stocks last

Later, imagining that I had bought these items, I mused as follows:

The £2 off for two bottles of gin increased the *size* of purchase, the question now is what effect it will have on the *frequency*. Presuming our home consumption of gin is neither compulsive nor routine, it is possible that we may get through it a little faster for having plenty around, or be less likely to have a period when we have none in stock. It might be worth it from the brand manager's perspective, though the discount is bigger than it seems in terms of forgone revenue, because of the excise duty included in the price.

It is difficult to see how buying the discounted luxury quilted toilet tissue will make any overall difference to our total consumption (!); it could represent a small triumph for the store manager who is temporarily increasing contribution if enough people go for a bigger spend. It depends upon how many people visit the store over an extended period – in the extreme case, if every shopper goes for it, next month's toilet tissue sales will be minimal. This suggests a straight swap – a 'trade-off' as it is known – between *size* of purchase at the expense of *frequency*.

Neither of these promotions is likely to increase the *penetration* – increasing my total spend on an item increases the perceived risk, which is the basic barrier to switching in the first place. The marked-down frozen stir-fry vegetables were designed as a *penetration* improvement. The idea made sense; indeed, it rang a bell, and when I got home, I discovered in the freezer a similar packet bought several months ago. The brand has some work to do on the frequency front.

The mini muesli seemed a great idea, a nice low risk, penetration attempt which might in turn lead to regular use of bigger size packs. Breakfast products are a complex area, since children have a large say as to which cereals appear on the table. I would speculate that variety packs have a pretty high *penetration* (that is, most households consume them at one time or another), but suffer from low purchase frequency compared to larger cereal packs because they are seen to be expensive. Therefore, this is probably a frequency attempt – to get variety packs back on the shopping list until someone decides they have to go – but there are additional complications, as the variety pack contains various brands each of which has its own independent – and potentially mind-boggling – status with its consumers.

The promotion of the fabric conditioner with the washing powder appears sensible. It is the practice of manufacturers not to identify themselves, so the choice of the preferred brand of powder acted as a guarantor for the conditioner, and – since conditioner is not essential – efforts which encourage its use are to be applauded. In contrast, it is difficult to reason out the dishwasher powder; who would buy a one kilo pack simply to get an additional 800 grams free, who would not buy the one kilo pack anyway?

Of course, the honey made sense. Thanks to the shelf display (and possibly the fact that I recognise 454 grams as 1 lb) I could see that the larger jar was cheaper (by 24%, though I only worked this out when I got home). I fancy that the large jar on the breakfast table may encourage overall consumption – though the price difference might just be a reflection of the relative costs of bringing them to the market. After all, honey actually costs nothing to make! If this is true, it represents a missed opportunity perhaps, for there is no reason why a price should relate to a cost, provided consumers will pay the price. With ready-to-eat jelly, I was left wondering if consumers will only pay 25p if that price appears to have been reduced from 35p. What exactly is the total purchasing proposition of a tub of ready-to-eat jelly?

Promotions

Reading the first draft of this chapter, my mentor queried whether the toilet tissue offer is an incentive to try a premium quality brand. Perhaps the price per roll in the offer is comparable with the regular price of a lower quality, but to me this seems too complicated an offer. I still have to fork out more money to try the better brand, so I think a better approach would be a trial pack at the same price as the usual purchase. Perhaps I am being too rational. Ultimately, the test is in what happens, about which there are usually a few problems of measurement and 'what if' calculations. Electronic checkout systems gather data with complete precision, of course, but the data belongs to the store. While it is increasingly being linked directly with suppliers, there are still difficulties in isolating local effects.

Mostly, the results are that with a promotion – as with most things – you, the promoter, get what you pay for. In other words, promotions may induce temporary switching or increased consumption, but the additional profit contribution is more or less offset by the cost of the activity, most of the time. Perhaps this answers a second observation about the draft – that there aren't enough positive examples of successes. The problem here is that success is not predictable – while potential failure might be. As described in Chapter 3, a consumer magazine group provides reader offers where it devotes space to publicising a special price it has negotiated with a supplier for featured goods, from the sale of which it receives a trading margin. Typically, the group earns from these what it would receive in advertising revenue for the space (and reckons it is benefiting its readers) but occasionally – and unpredictably – one of the offers really captures the readers' imagination. Such unpredictability is typical.

As far as a formula for guaranteed success is concerned, there isn't one, and there are three good reasons why not. Firstly, persistent success would mean that consumers are stupid; secondly, other brands would copy what was being done and neutralise the incentive; and thirdly, anyone who had such a formula would be most unlikely to publish it. The reason for not publishing 'success stories' at great length is enshrined in the second point above. People are only too willing to copy what they see their competitors and colleagues doing, but they do not always do so carefully enough. They should consider all the details to ensure that a proposal is appropriate to their own circumstances. Even if the promotion is entirely based on emotional responses, it still requires an underlying logic, and this can only be tested by reference to first principles, those of consumer behaviour.

The most famous, or infamous, failure to consider the circumstances fully was the Hoover promotion of 1992. It is not unusual for domestic appliances to be sold with apparently major incentives attached, such as free or cheap flights. With infrequent purchases, there is no brand 'switching'. Being first is everything, so the incentive is worth it if it wins the sale at a competitor's expense. There are two usual conditions, however: the consumer was going to buy the appliance anyway; and the bonus offer proves rather hard to realise, requiring someone to take a 6am flight from Prestwick airport at two days' notice, or some such thing. In these circumstances, purchasers do not proceed to convert the offer, with the promoters reckoning that any ill will should disappear from the equation by the time the next purchase is to be made, which could be five years away. Hoover therefore used figures in its calculations based upon these usual conversion rates, when it proceeded to offer free air tickets to the USA for anyone who spent more than £100 on a

Hoover product. The result is well known. Depending on how you look at it, this was one of the worst – or best – consumer promotions ever seen. The plain fact was – it was worth buying an appliance simply to obtain the air ticket, so the conversion rate remained close to 100%. Unused vacuum cleaners became so common at car boot sales that perplexed police would telephone retailers asking if they had been burgled. It is true that Hoover had to step up vacuum cleaner production as a result of this, but it also had to deal with rather a large number of complaints about the provision of the free tickets, spend around £50 million providing the free flights much later than promised, and dispense with the services of three senior executives.

Back on a normal plane, my visit to this supermarket does not show in any sales statistics as I did not actually buy anything, nor did I accumulate any points in its loyalty scheme. Individual consumer decisions about which FMCG stores to visit are frequently taken, and the same pattern of behaviour is observed as with products themselves. Over time, modest incentives are insufficient to change brand shares, and the probability is very much that store loyalty schemes will not last. They have an impact in the short term, but unless consumers both perceive and experience good value from them, their importance will fade. In any case, if every store has a scheme, it will be possible for any consumer to belong to them all. There is no exclusion clause. As long as they are thought to be successful, every store *will* have a scheme, which can only mean that individual schemes will have to get better and better to compete for customers. This in turn means that schemes will cost stores more and more, and eventually too much. After a suitable time has passed for embarrassment to be avoided, a spokesperson for one retailer will announce that they have decided to suspend their scheme, and the industry, breathing a collective sigh of relief, will follow suit. Long live the consumer!

WHERE TO NEXT?

Advertising helps brands (Chapter 2)
Price offers tend to reduce profits (Chapter 5)
The predictability of demand helps the gearing decision (Chapter 15)
Information about behaviour is only the beginning of the decision (Chapter 17)

10. The marketing mix – 4Ps and 5Cs

Selling things repeatedly, over time, *requires an understanding of all the factors influencing buyer behaviour, inside and outside the business*

Marketing involves understanding consumer choice, which is the reason why there is no proper Russian word for it. They call it *mar-kyet-eeng*. Before *perestroika*, there was no need for such a word because there was no consumer choice, officially. In a market economy, choice exists wherever people set out to buy something, and the term *marketing mix* refers to the 'cocktail of ingredients' available for a firm to offer its customers. Like a recipe, it is the proportions and manner in which the ingredients are mixed that produce the desired result. This applies to basic meals as much as to *haute cuisine*. To demonstrate the marketing mix in action, consider not a leading branded consumer product, but the services of a plumber. In doing so, we need to consider how *most people* behave when they buy plumbing services. This is not to say that everyone behaves this way, and if you are one of the exceptions, please think of some other example to help visualise the scene.

The plumbing market

People require plumbers in differing circumstances. In an emergency – frozen pipes, or a boiler threatening to explode – all that matters is *getting one*. From the plumber's perspective, *delivery* is everything. The customers may start by phoning one they know, but then out will come Yellow Pages: the most local plumbers will be tried first, but the one who answers, 'We'll be round immediately,' will be the one who gets the order. All will deny there is a call-out charge (though there is, in effect) and the question, 'How much will it be?' will be answered with, 'That depends on the work to be done.' It will be expensive for what it is, based on a rate per hour which would make the plumber a fortune, if only he could get a full week's work. (He can't, of course.) The fact that the customer regards the sum as exorbitant is not a problem (except that it is up to the plumber to collect it there and then); they will not be meeting again in the short term, for in a repeat of the emergency the customer will not try the same plumber again, at least, not with any intention of paying.

In entirely different circumstances, the same family may decide they want a second bathroom to cater for the increasing sophistication of their children. In this case, they will ask friends to recommend plumbers they have used. Such events are infrequent, and the plumber therefore depends upon his *reputation* to secure further introductions. The customer will invite the plumber to visit the house and prepare an estimate. This may be to compare alternative prices, or just to agree a price in advance. The customer's main concern is *quality* – that the plumber will do a good job – though perceptions of quality may be based more on appearance, tidiness, punctuality etc than actual pipework. The rate per hour will be lower than the emergency man's, but the overall job will cost more.

Not all plumbing is done for individuals, and one of the construction managers of a new housing development will be responsible for hiring subcontractors who will plumb in the bathrooms etc. It is unlikely that a person working alone would get this contract, but for the sake of symmetry, let us suppose that someone does. He may be invited to tender, with the lowest price obtaining the job other than in exceptional circumstances. Indeed, the buyer will know exactly how much he is prepared to pay and will invite tenders from plumbers he knows, because reliability will matter. There is an overall building schedule, and it will be important for the plumbing not to delay other work. For the buyer, completion on time, and to budget, are the main considerations. The price per hour will be less than the bathroom builder, as the subcontract plumber does not have to cover the other hours spent visiting possible jobs and issuing estimates. The overall contract will be more valuable.

From a marketing perspective, the three plumbers have different *propositions* to offer; people choose to purchase according to the *benefits* they require. The alleviation of threat or discomfort, smoother morning routines eventually (and reassurance over physical disruption in the short term), or the successful completion of another development and proper fulfilment of a job, are the respective benefits in this case, involving not just tangible aspects – the actual pipework – but also intangible considerations relating to people's feelings. It is theoretically possible for the same person to need a plumber in all three circumstances; the subcontract buyer might not want the people he knows from sitework having access to his home, and in an emergency, anyone will do. In contrast, it is improbable that the plumber can be more than one of these at the same time, since the price charged is part of the overall proposition put to the customer. The degree of flexibility in *price* depends upon its relative importance in the *purchasing decisions*, where it is considered in combination with *quality* and *delivery* issues. This also involves the non-pipework aspects of the *proposition* – how the plumber behaves – which are roughly the equivalent of the *packaging* for a physical *product*.

The form the plumber's *promotional* work takes is determined by the behaviour of his target customer, which is greatly affected by the customer's *frequency of purchase*. In the subcontract case, the sensible plumber will maintain good relationships with the few important people in the broad vicinity who have the big jobs to offer. Whatever activity and expenditure this entails, it will not involve *advertising* in Yellow Pages and other directories, which are the emergency plumber's lifeline (though the clamour to get to the front of the list and make the biggest impact leads to a certain overkill in the plumbing section – have a look). The domestic bathroom plumber may do a little advertising locally, insert cards or leaflets through letter-boxes, and generally maintain a local presence with smart vehicles and premises, but in the main, he will depend upon *referrals* from satisfied customers.

Without defining precisely the marketing mix, this example demonstrates how various activities along different dimensions contribute together to the way in which revenue is generated. Words such as price, promotion, purchasing pattern, packaging, product, proposition, are all what you would expect to find in a marketing text, though their all beginning with the letter P is something of a coincidence.

The 4Ps

Perhaps it was the prevalence of words beginning with P which caused someone to nominate the 4Ps as defining the marketing mix:

Product
Price
Promotion
Place

The first three are straightforward, but what do you make of Place? In some cases, it is actually equivalent to 'location' – for retail businesses, of course. For manufacturers, it also means retailers, but not so much their location as their price-quality profile. It may also include the businesses who supply the retailers. For insurance companies, it could mean telephone call centres, representatives, or brokers.

It represents a superb example of the marketing profession shooting itself in the foot. It is fine and dandy for everything to begin with P for appearance's sake – but not if Place really stands for *Channels of Distribution*. It does – and it under-emphasises their significance.

The 4Ps have their uses, but like most checklists, they should be applied carefully, after first ensuring that the context is appropriate. Consider, for example, a branded blended drink like Dubonnet. In France, the Ps might describe it as: 'A premium priced aperitif for discerning palates, promoted via sophisticated magazine features, available through quality wine merchants and specialist restaurant suppliers.' In England, however, the same 'product' might warrant this description: 'A drink for infrequent female pub visitors, distributed via the main brewers, with advertising only justified for pre-Christmas sales through the independent off-trade'. Many mistakes have been made trying to take products across national boundaries while assuming the mix will stay the same. The Ps tell the main facts about how the brand sells in each market, but there is no clue as to the difference between the two marketplaces, which derives from the perceptions of the consumer.

People encountering the 4Ps for the first time can be excused for assuming that if *Place* refers to the store in which you can obtain something, then *Positioning*[1] must refer to the supermarket shelf on which you find it. This demonstrates the interconnectedness of the mix well; unfortunately, it is incorrect. The P that should determine the shelf is *Product*, being that which defines the benefits offered to the consumer. *Positioning* is what relates the product to alternatives on offer, both within the supplier's own portfolio, and in the context of competitive products. According to some theorists, positioning refers to where the item is 'located' within the consumer's perception, or rather, where the marketer attempts to locate it.

This typifies the rather unthinking, self-centred outlook inherent in the Ps. Where someone locates a particular item within their perception is firstly determined by their own personality, and secondly, a function of their perceptions of similar, alternative items offered for sale by competitors. It is a major criticism of the Ps that competitors rank so low in the list of things to think about. Indeed, there is nothing in the 4Ps which even alludes to competition, though it is the very essence of the market economy.

Buyer behaviour

The Ps can be thought of as *inside-out.* They start with the marketing department at 'the centre of the universe' looking out on the world, mixing variables to project outwards at some chosen target. The approach is like shining a spotlight; it provides a close-up on the subject and its immediate surroundings, but in doing so loses definition of the wider context. There are significant differences between social patterns in France and England which affect the consumption of alcoholic drinks, including where, when, and even why. These should be recognised first, because the chances are a brand manager cannot change them single-handed.

All good marketing decisions begin with an analysis of customer buying behaviour, for it is influenced by many factors, not always obvious, and usually expensive and difficult to change. Starting this way provides an *outside-in* approach, with observations about customers being used to generate a range of

---

[1] Some teachers add this word as the fifth P when discussing consumer products.

options which the brand manager may choose from. The checklist which reflects this outside-in approach is the 5Cs.

The 5 Cs

These are:

Consumers
Channels
Competitors
Communication
Costs

'Customer', as you can see, is not one of these Cs. For anything that is sold several times in a supply chain, the end user is the biggest influence in events along the stream, so the first of the Cs is the *consumer.* Consumers are reached through *channels of distribution* which have their own expectations of and interests in the process. The shaping of consumer alternatives and channel structures is heavily influenced by the firm's *competitors.* Considering these factors is like surveying the wider environment, *after* which it may be useful to shine the spotlight of the 4 or more Ps. This may be broadly represented by the theme of *communication*, which represents the firm's own contribution to changing (or maintaining) the status quo. The final element of the equation is the *cost* involved. With a big enough budget, you can more or less sell anything to anyone, but no one ever has a big enough budget.

Consumer satisfaction

In essence, the 5Cs acknowledge that 'you cannot fool all of the people all of the time'. Both scientific observation and everyday experience show that people simply do not carry on buying a particular thing unless they derive satisfaction from its consumption. This satisfaction exists in a number of dimensions, and the image alone of a product is not sufficient to overcome defects in its performance. It is not easy to create satisfaction. It can be argued that many consumer products are not exactly necessary; it is undeniably true that most innovations do not succeed in pleasing the consumer, and consequently fail. Whatever your personal opinion about items on supermarket shelves, the probability is strongly that their presence there means plenty of other people like them.

For generations, Guinness ran highly creative advertising campaigns for its close-to-unique brew, campaigns which achieved the highest recall ratings, and which by and large the public found entertaining and charming. Yet, when it came to the crunch, the number of people drinking the brew regularly did not increase – for the rather fundamental reason that a large proportion of people do not like the taste of Guinness.[2]

The public's demand for a reliable taste is what is thought to have caused the great *volte face* at Coca-Cola when the new recipe was withdrawn within a few days of its launch (though the alacrity with which this happened suggests something more subtle may have been taking place). It may be that the taste of Coca-Cola has actually changed subtly over the years (and it is quite impossible to prove of course), in line with changes in taste generally; yet, not even Coke's massive advertising budget could persuade consumers to accept an abrupt change.

Consumer satisfaction is of direct importance to the manufacturer when the product is a frequent purchase. When it is infrequent, the individual consumer's ability to experiment and decide on preference by trial and error is more or less removed, particularly for expensive things. Unscrupulous manufacturers might consider selling less than effective products (and historically they have done), but it is the relationship with the distribution channels which brings about fair deals.

Given that the marketing mix is a holistic concept *par excellence*, it will not be a surprise that its components have been discussed at length in other chapters. Chapter 9 is essentially about consumer behaviour for frequently-purchased goods, and forms of communication are discussed in Chapters 2 and 3, together with the issue of costs. Reference to competitors is implicit throughout, most obviously where they influence pricing options (Chapter 5), or consumer's expectations of price,

---

[2] Guinness advertising did work in the short term. Its high appeal would sometimes result in temporary increased sales of other Irish stouts in pubs which did not stock the big brand, one indication of the obvious fact that if you cannot get your product to the consumer, your advertising will achieve little. Hence the importance of channels.

delivery and quality combinations, for example (Chapter 8). The section on research (Chapter 18) tells of the importance of learning what competitors are doing. This leaves *channels of distribution* for further discussion.

Channels

Channels of distribution convert occasional, sporadic transactions between *producers* at one end of a chain and *consumers* at the other into regular trading relationships between *customers and suppliers.* An appliance manufacturer will not sell a washing machine to an individual more often than once every few years (and will find the cost of maintaining interim communications prohibitive), but will supply a store like Curry's on a very frequent basis. The individual may not have quite the same repeat relationship with the retailer, but transactions may be more common across a broad range of products, and the cost of maintaining contact through catalogues etc is justified. Moreover, if the customer is unsatisfied with the purchase, the retailer will be the first to know. For this reason, the unscrupulous manufacturers mentioned earlier have usually operated door-to-door. The manufacturer-retailer-consumer version is the simplest form of channel; more complex versions exist, as in manufacturer-exporter-importer-dealer-consumer for automobiles for example – and the spare parts might possibly follow a different channel. The word *distribution* has a commercial rather than a necessarily logistical meaning. The physical movement of goods may well be contracted to a third party, as a study of motorway traffic will indicate. In the late 1990s, management appointments frequently appear for 'relationship marketing' and 'supply chain management' posts, showing a recognition within organisations of the long-term importance of channels.

It follows that two sets of forces determine the transactions that take place: firstly, the products must be appropriate to the needs, tastes. and purchasing patterns of the *consumers* at the end of a channel; secondly, the terms of the transaction must satisfy the commercial interests of each of the *customer* members. It is not enough for the product to be suitable for the customer's customers. The commercial terms must also be acceptable, such as prices and margins/discounts, payment terms, delivery arrangements, promotion plans etc. There is also a mutual need for *reliability*. Suppliers will require the customers to put appropriate effort into promoting their lines. Customers will want to know that if they do this, there will be a regular supply of goods available of this price and quality.

The relationships within a channel are of a permanent nature, and, for human as well as economic reasons, are not renegotiated each time there is a transaction. (Such permanent preferences can be found even in near-perfect markets.) The *overall costs* of the transactions in a channel are important. The supplier needs to balance the discounts etc granted against what it might cost to sell products in other ways. The customer will be aware that there are potential risks and costs involved in switching to a new supplier.

Channels and competition

It is very difficult to compete where there are high supplier-customer 'replacement' costs. Offering marginal benefits is usually insufficient incentive to induce a change from a satisfactory relationship. A manufacturer with powerful channels in place has an easier task therefore introducing a new product than a weak competitor, and a new business finds it hardest of all.

Maximum profitability in terms of return on marketing effort is achieved through selecting those channels which provide greatest volume for least promotional support. Manufacturers seeking maximum market share objectives will tend to pursue many channels, in order to reach most consumers. Members of parallel channels may be in competition with each other, of course, and this could involve competing on the range of brands carried and suppliers represented. Hence, it may not be possible to supply all available channels.[3] This is an important factor in markets based upon so-called tied outlets such as petrol and beer. No matter how powerful their relationship with consumers brands in such markets are restricted in their choice of channels. 'Owning' (exercising effective influence over) strong channels is

---

[3] If there are no choices of channel, there is a monopoly for one distributor, which is a generally undesirable situation for everyone except shareholders in the monopoly.

arguably worth more than owning a range of powerful brands (although neither is much use without the other). The latter are subject to life-cycles, fashion changes, etc, whereas with good management the former can last indefinitely.

Channels are also important in markets where the consumers are organisations. Compared to people-markets, there will in general be fewer consumers, and their purchasing decisions will be more complex. The manufacturer's ability to 'pull' things through the chain by advertising to consumers may be different, but the same considerations generally apply to intra- and inter-channel relationships.

Balance of power

Who holds sway – and therefore might wish to take the lion's share of the profits – in the channel is an important consideration. In a well-balanced market, the supplier will have a product, differentiated from alternatives by its function and/or brand, which the customer really cannot afford to risk not stocking; the customer meanwhile will offer access to a group of consumers that the supplier cannot easily reach by other means. The balance for fast moving consumer goods has probably swung in favour of retailers, away from the once all-powerful manufacturers with irresistible brands. Occasionally, it has been tested, such as when the Asda supermarket chain in the north of England decided its domination was such that it would not bother to stock Weetabix (on grounds of the high transaction costs involved in dealing with a 'small' supplier). The loss of the channel was sufficient to render Weetabix's advertising campaign in the region too costly; fortunately, the local consumers stepped into the breach, or rather, voted with their feet, and the decision was rescinded. The chances are you will now be able to buy Weetabix at your nearest Asda.

WHERE TO NEXT?

After 4 Ps and 5 Cs, try 6 Ms (Chapter 3)
The mix also applies in the service sector (Chapter 8)
Generating revenue creates the top line, from which the bottom is calculated (Chapter 16)
Researching competitors is invaluable (Chapter 18)

11. The essence of strategy

Strategy is about deciding ***what business you want to be in****. Management is about staying in it*

A firm's strategy is based on its long-term view of the future. *Strategic planning* sets out the overall purpose of the enterprise, and the objectives it will pursue. Through adopting defined strategies, large firms set out to shape the environment around them, exploiting the opportunities which they calculate will best enable them to out-perform their competitors. Strategies are not easily or regularly changed, or managers would not know what they were supposed to be doing. It is the existence of strategies which – when translated into actions at the working level – enable employees to realise more or less literally what day of the week it is. They can come in each morning and get on with their work. If a course of action isn't working out as expected, you do not blame the strategy, you change the way it is implemented.

A colleague used to refer to large firms as farmers, shaping their environment over the long term, husbanding customers and creating demand where none previously existed. Small firms are hunter-gatherers, content or perhaps with no choice but to patrol their surroundings looking for available foodstuffs. In the sense of shaping the future, small firms indeed lack the resources in most circumstances, but they still pursue strategies. Just as hunter-gatherers might develop special skills in harvesting fruit, recognising fungi, or tracking certain animal prey, so small firm owner-managers develop and maintain specialist skills in seeking out customers for unusual processes, or solving special problems.

It is possible that some firms are not aware explicitly of their chosen strategy, as it may have evolved over a long period of time in response to events in the marketplace. There are famous examples of 'implicit' strategies, such as a major UK construction firm which only appointed a corporate planning department after the founder had died and no one could any longer say, 'we can't do that, the guv'nor won't approve.' These days, most organisations will have mission statements and associated corporate plans, even when they are not businesses.

The pursuit of defined strategies can have some disadvantages as well. Promising business opportunities may be allowed to pass by if they do not fit into a strategy, and this is a restriction on opportunistic or entrepreneurial activities. *Entrepreneur* may be a word with more subtleties of meaning than strategy; perhaps one definition is: someone who is willing to sacrifice strategic plans in favour of unexpected opportunities. This would be one reason why entrepreneurs and large organisations do not mix well.

Survival and success

The effect of world economic cycles of boom and recession in the last decades has been for strategy to take two apparent forms. During recessions, firms look to the core businesses to protect them; they decide what businesses they are best at running and concentrate on them. In the 1990s recession, this approach was known as 'core competences' to distinguish it from the effectively identical 'sticking to your knitting' approach of the eighties.

During booms, firms seek to grow faster than the core businesses will permit, so they diversify, frequently, though not always, by acquisition. In simple terms, diversifying means selling new products to new customers, and if a firm is to have any control over how it does this, it will seek to apply the same 'competences' in the new product-market that it uses in its existing field. In this respect, the strategic planning process follows the same principles, except that it looks at opportunities outside the current sphere.

There is another approach to diversification, which applies at a rarefied level where the firm decides that it knows how to run businesses which operate according to certain criteria, even if it does not understand the underlying trading activity. For example, Sainsbury set up Homebase because it reckoned that running large DIY stores provided many opportunities for it to use its established competences in retailing. The Ladbroke Group operated Texas Homecare from a base of running betting shops and hotels, businesses which do not sell products from shelves (and certainly have nothing to do with home improvements), presumably because they knew how to run businesses based on cash-paying customers at branch units with highly-routinised decision making. Thus, we should distinguish between business strategy – how the firm *runs its business* – and corporate strategy, which is about running businesses *on an aggregate level*.

There is a hint above of a fashion cycle in the world of strategy. I spoke recently to a respected colleague who told me that core competences are 'old hat, but I'm not sure what the latest is'. This is probably a good enough reason for leaving the subject of corporate strategy alone, but it is in any case enough for our purposes to understand strategy at the business level. At the time of writing, the merger between Grand Metropolitan and Guinness is still awaiting approval by the authorities. GrandMet really came to prominence in the 1960s through its acquisition of breweries. It disposed of them in 1990, so there is something potentially puzzling about its desire to merge with another brewer. Similar questions might be asked about why Hanson plc considered it appropriate in 1996 to dispose by demerger of Imperial Tobacco which it acquired through a hostile bid in 1986, and why BTR can spend most of the 1980s acquiring businesses only to dispose of them through the 1990s. Perhaps such perplexities help to make corporate strategy a popular subject. There are lots of books on it – which is interesting because there are actually very few people in any corporation in a position really to influence corporate strategy. Business strategy is another matter, for it involves everyone in the firm.

Business strategy

This is about organising the various functions within an enterprise to achieve the same set of objectives, which have been identified as the directions in which the business wishes to develop. In that sense, the whole of this book is about strategy at work, since everything should relate to the general premise that *a business must sell things repeatedly, over time, for more money than it spends in so doing.* The strategic planning process for a firm is about deciding what these things will be, and to whom they will be sold; the consequent how, where, and so on, are the essence of good management. History has a big part to say in the answers to these questions, but that little bit extra which makes the difference – those few pence of earnings per share which the chairman has promised shareholders – comes from strategy.

Identifying the things and the customers at the same time introduces the product-market concept, something central – but often overlooked – in the 'classical' approach to strategy developed by H. Igor Ansoff.[1] Any firm operates in an *environment* which is not static but *dynamic*, being in the broadest sense influenced by *political, economic, social and technological* factors, which need to be examined. This is the so-called PEST (or STEP) analysis. Within this environment, the firm operates in a number of *product-markets*, as do its various competitors. The concept of product-market is crucial, defining the firm's activities not just by what it sells, but also to whom it sells the 'what'. Statistical classification of industries usually involves one or the other, but both are needed. A manufacturer of animal foodstuffs is in the same productive arena as a major bread producer, but not the same market; it is in the same market as a tractor manufacturer, but not the same industry.

For each of its product-markets, the firm may compare itself with its competitors, in terms of its relative *strengths and weaknesses.* This can be difficult to do objectively, and has given rise to the concept of *benchmarking* – finding out what others achieve to make direct comparisons. At the same time, anticipated events and trends in the environment raise the prospect of *opportunities* for growth or new product-markets, and *threats* to existing business. The examination of strengths, weaknesses, opportunities and threats is known as SWOT analysis.

SWOT seeks to identify product-markets in which the firm has a *comparative advantage* over its competitors, and these are the key business activities in which the firm should concentrate. It should then endeavour to protect its superiority through the building and reinforcement of economic *barriers to entry.* The

---

[1] Ansoff's book is called *Corporate Strategy* (McGraw-Hill, 1965), but it also deals with business strategy. The distinction lies in the bottom corner of the famous matrix which plots existing and new markets against existing and new missions. Corporate strategy – otherwise known as diversification – starts with the new-new cell.

origins of comparative advantage can be explained in part by economic factors such as *economies of scale* in production, research and development, or frequently, marketing and distribution. It can derive from intangible but definite factors such as the ownership of intellectual property rights (patents, trade marks etc). It can also be because one firm is simply better at certain things than its competitors. This 'being better' is termed *distinctive competence*.

That this is the same root as the modern *core competence* should not come as a surprise, since specialisation is as old as firms themselves.[2] As discussed in Chapter 16, when a firm forecasts that it will make a superior profit, the question should be: why? If this question can be answered satisfactorily and objectively (and it is not based on some innate belief such as 'we have never failed yet'), then the particular procedure chosen for the analysis is unimportant.

Checking for consistency

There are definite criteria that strategic analysis should satisfy, which happen to provide the mnemonics of CAR and VAN. Firstly any strategy must be *Coherent* – all parts of the strategic unit must be covered by it, and they must subscribe to it, in the sense of adopting the set of priorities the strategy determines. Secondly, the strategy needs to *Anticipate*. Events which throw the strategy into turmoil should not normally be unexpected. Without developing a plan for every contingency, the strategy should be able to cope with most foreseeable events. Thirdly, it should be *Relevant*, being based firmly in the external environment, and not reflecting some obscure scheme which sounds good in the boardroom but means nothing to customers and ignores competition.

In order to deliver a strategy which satisfies these criteria, the organisation needs a source of *Vision*. It has to have a concept of the time beyond its current working horizons, of how one day things might become different from how they are currently seen. Otherwise, management will tend to expect the

---

[2] The idea of specialisation is usually attributed to Adam Smith. If you are even tempted to quote him, remember the full title of the book is *An Inquiry into the Nature and Causes of the Wealth of Nations*.

future to be much the same. If it did not have this tendency, there would be no need for the expression 'management of change'. This vision has then to be integrated with current activities, through a process of *Articulation*, a word with connotations of both flexible links and verbal explanation. The corporate mission statement might be vague, as in 'to be the best supplier of left-handed prummets to the fosset industry', but via the strategy, people actually employed in supplying prummets should know that the way they do something is not 'because that's how we've always done it' but 'because it helps us to be the best'. They should also be willing to change to stay the best. Finally, everyone should have a responsibility for keeping up-to-date and informing others, through a process of *Networking*. This is a slightly over-used word, currently running the risk of hijack by the IT industry. As well as covering internal communication (for which successfully networked computers or an intranet are a promising option) it is equally as important outside the organisation. Customers can be a very useful source of information about what competitors are doing and other industry events, of course, but so can suppliers and service companies.

Problems of interpretation

In a famous article called 'Marketing Myopia', Ted Levitt argued that firms need to operate with a much broader perspective of the marketplace in which they compete. He quoted the example of Penn Central Railroad, which had gone bankrupt because, by considering itself a railroad company, it had failed to notice competition from airlines for its customers. If it had thought of itself as in the transportation business, it would have behaved differently. The arguments are seemingly convincing, and all very well, but – if your assets are in track and stations and locomotives and rolling stock – it is very difficult to fly. Some years later, data from the Strategic Planning Institute in Cambridge Massachusetts may have indicated that firms actually do better when they define their markets narrowly.[3]

---

[3] The PIMS (profit impact of marketing strategies) analysed data supplied by a large number of participating firms, and identified a

The indisputable point is that competition may come from further afield; the environment needs to be watched at all times.

Continuing the transport theme, an unusual possession of mine is the horn from a Morris Traveller *circa* 1960, which I removed when the car was abandoned after a highly satisfactory career. The horn had a throaty roar reminiscent of an ocean liner, and I intended to fit it into another vehicle, only to find that this was impossible. The Morris version is a diecast metal hemisphere connected to something which actually resembles a section of a horn, coiled across the plane surface (which perhaps accounts for the sound). It weighs 1.4 kilos and occupies about 5 litres of space, whereas its modern equivalent weighs in at 300 grams and half a litre, resembling a small loudspeaker. It is to be hoped that the horn manufacturer (who would have been a subcontractor) recognised the threat when motor cars started to be made with emphasis on space and weightsaving as epitomised by the Traveller's little sister, the Mini. From the product-market perspective of supplying diecast components to the motor industry, the threat posed by shifts in customer specification should have been apparent, though there is something about the design of the actual horn which suggests that the vision to redefine the task – and thus the technology – was not vested in its producer.

People often seem to encounter difficulty undertaking a SWOT analysis on the business they are very close to. They can identify a factor as simultaneously a strength and a weakness, and they mix up internal considerations (which are S or W) and interpret them as Os or Ts. The corporate plan for a design consultancy (which will be anonymous for obvious reasons) once read as follows: *Our Leader* is a Strength, because he knows the industry well etc; *Our Leader* is a Weakness because he handles all the clients and has limited time; *Our Leader* is an Opportunity, because his style is popular; *Our Leader* is a

---

correlation between share of market and level of return on investment, something which helped encourage the pursuit of market share. The analysis did not identify causal factors, but one interpretation – given that only relatively few firms can have the highest market share under broad definitions – was that those firms which defined their markets most tightly tended to be the more profitable.

Threat, because if his reputation is damaged, we are doomed.[4]

Opportunities and Threats are always external probabilities and possibilities, and the firm interprets them in light of its ability to respond, up to and including the decision to contribute to the encouragement of a particular trend. The advent of compact disc technology was undoubtedly a T to anyone owning a vinyl record-pressing plant, needing a radical response to stay in business. It was not hard to identify as an O for record stores, because the new format opened the market for massive retrospective sales as people converted their vinyl collections. Fifty years ago, the marketplace for popular music sales was different. 'Hit Parades' were based upon sheet music sales, and those retailers who saw the widespread growth of gramophone records as a threat were correct – but only those who saw them as an opportunity survived.

Thirty years ago there was a firm called Timesharing UK Ltd; it owned mainframe computers the use of which was shared by its customers who would dispatch their punch cards in the evening and receive processed transactions in the morning (the computers had no memory). The firm's strategy was to grow rapidly as it believed that computers would become bigger and bigger in physical size, and more given to timesharing than to ownership by end users. Computing facilities would thus become a utility network like telephones, and because of its strategic importance to the British nation, the network would be nationalised, with the biggest firms receiving the greatest compensation. As we now know, computers have become ever smaller; end users own their machines (in fact, children own machines); computing has not become a utility; UK utilities have been privatised; and timesharing means that someone owns the right in perpetuity to occupy an apartment in the Canary Islands for the first week of November.

The words 'how wrong can you be?' come to mind, yet the future with regard to computing is no clearer; witness the debate

---

[4] It is tempting to add that *Our Leader* is probably a pain in the neck. His reputation is probably a strength; his handling of all the clients is a weakness in the management structure which the firm will have to rectify if it wants to grow. The popularity of his designs is likely to be a function of current trends, and is only an opportunity for as long as these trends continue to favour his style. As for the threat, no doubt the end of the world is also bad news for the firm.

between Microsoft and Oracle in 1995 at the Paris Conference, at which Bill Gates and Larry Ellison vociferously defended their visions of the future of computing through PCs versus Networks. There is always a need for a vision of the future, otherwise how can a business think ahead? There was a theme of 'chaos' popular in between the last two recessions which claimed that the world was changing too rapidly for strategies to be much use. Well, an objective of being 'flexible, adaptive and responsive so as to exploit rapid change' seems a perfectly acceptable plank of a strategy. Where the strategic approach can be criticised is when it is assumed that events are etched in stone once a strategy has been defined. Firms put their heads over the parapet and survey the surroundings, only to sink back down again and subsequently ignore what the enemy (= competitors) are doing.

Environmental analysis is open to all, so that many players can anticipate the same demographic trend, for example. When Sainsbury identified Homebase, roughly speaking, Ladbroke Group identified Texas Homecare, W H Smith started Do It All, and Ward White (subsequently acquired by Boots) Payless-DIY; Kingfisher (aka Woolworth) expanded B & Q, and so on. All these firms appeared to pursue the same generic strategy, of creating market share in a growing sector by building out-of-town superstores. Defining market share by capacity – ie floor selling area – favoured large-scale developments, even though sites were difficult to come by and the pace of store openings slow. The players avoided head-on competition by differentiating their consumer propositions somewhat, and for a long time they withstood the temptation to compete on price. Probably the splendid margins on which they operated kept them all going through the 1980s,[5] but they all ignored the basic problem – that there were too many of them. Not only that, but demand was not going to grow for ever; a major chunk of it was generated by the demographic phenomenon of the post-war baby boom, which found people obliged to undertake DIY at certain, finite, stages of their lives which have now passed. Not one of these firms –

[5] DIY 'sheds' always gave the impression that because they resembled supermarkets they were somehow cheap. This is not so; commodities like nails, sold elsewhere loose by weight, are packaged and sold at considerable margins. Most consumers are infrequent purchasers, and would not know this.

each successful in other respects – was able to take stock of what the others were doing and respond by switching to a programme of say, rapid acquisition of small neighbourhood hardware stores which could be rapidly packaged into some corporate formula and steal the lion's share of the market from under the others' noses.[6]

However, this observation is made with the benefit of hindsight, a tool not available to corporate planners. There is no guarantee that a firm will choose its strategy correctly; what is fairly certain, is that once it has chosen, it will 'stick to its guns'. This is a tremendous opportunity for firms who undertake continual competitor analysis.

WHERE TO NEXT?

All marketing messages should fit strategy (Chapter 3)
Matching operations to customer needs is sensible (Chapter 6)
Depreciation policy should be related to strategic expectations (Chapter 13)
In the final analysis, success comes down to people knowing what they are doing (Chapter 20)

---

[6] Ladbroke turned loss-making Texas around to project a small profit and sold it to Sainsbury in 1995. It then exited retailing. In 1996, Sainsbury announced its first ever fall in (underlying) profits – though it did not blame the acquisition. W H Smith merged Do It All with Boots' Payless in 1990. The combined group continued to make losses, and Smith 'sold out' its share to Boots in 1996 by giving the latter £63m (a new concept in payless-ness, perhaps). B & Q has continued, but it is a core business for Kingfisher.

12. Growing new ventures

New ventures obviously do not satisfy the criteria of Chapter 1, so their ultimate agenda is in front of them

It was Scott Fitzgerald who told us that the rich were different from the rest of us – by virtue of having more money. Writing in *Harvard Business Review*, Welsh and White told us that a small business is not a little business. *HBR* sells individual reprints of successful articles as student readings, and for a while, this one held the sales record. To this pool of wisdom, let us add the observation that a new business is different from an established one. Understanding the basis for this truism is very helpful in learning about how to approach new business ideas, for as someone else observed, a problem well-stated is halfway to a solution.

Starting with our definition – that an established business sells things repeatedly, over time, for more money than it spends in so doing – we conclude that a new business does not do this. There can be only a few reasons why. Firstly, it may not sell things; indeed, the moment before it starts, it does not sell things; *customers* are the issue. Next, it may not sell things repeatedly, because it sells to the wrong people, or what it sells is no good; this would suggest a problem of *competence.* It could also fail to sell things over time – that is, exhaust itself with the initial effort – because it lacked suitable *capacity.* Finally, it could sell things for less money than it spends in so doing, broadly speaking – a problem of *cash.*

Normally when someone wants to start a new business, there is this problem: 'If only I had the cash, I could invest it in the things I need which will give me the capacity so that I can then find customers. I am sure I am competent to do it.' The response of the typical bank manager to this observation is: 'Show me some customers. Then I will know that you are competent, and lend you the money to provide your capacity.' This is what we call a *vicious circle.*

Squaring the circle

Finding a way of overcoming the barrier of the vicious circle can involve people in years of work, sometimes to no avail or, arguably worse still, for them to watch the opportunity they have spotted disappear into the competitive marketplace. There is a general reluctance on the part of third parties to invest in business start-ups, and this is deemed in some quarters to be an inefficiency in the capital markets, known as the equity gap. This concept implies that there *ought* to be capital available, and it has been around a long time, having first been identified by a Royal Commission *circa* 1930. Other people take the view that this is the marketplace at work, and true entrepreneurs will succeed in getting started come what may. Those who think it would be better for the national economy if new ventures could raise capital more easily bemoan the disappearance of 'Aunt Agatha', who notionally used to indulge favourite nephews and nieces in their enterprises. We can be pretty certain that Agatha did not bother asking for a business plan. Whether the nation wants more new businesses starting without plans is a debatable issue.

In fact, the penniless aspirant[1] has only two places to turn these days – to a partner, or to a plan. The involvement of partners is a tricky affair which can lead to its own set of difficulties, and for some people it is out of the question. The motivation to start the business is sometimes purely opportunist, in the pursuit of profit, but more often it stems from a psychological desire. This can take the form of self-expression, or self-determination perhaps, and involve a scenario which essentially excludes partners. In consequence, it becomes the job of the business plan to square up to the vicious circle, and attempt a breakthrough at one or more of the four 'corners' of its construction.

In the context of new ventures, a business plan differs from a corporate plan in that the latter has the advantage of being based in fact rather than surmise. There are past and current year figures to support projections which in the business plan are purely speculative. The chances are, also, that the projected figures will be fairly similar to last year's. This is one of the

[1] This is a relative term. What matters is not having enough money for the desired purpose.

respects in which a (new) small business is not a little big business – its projections will be significantly different from the current (zero) position. The business plan is foretelling something which, even if it is rather small compared to General Motors, will nevertheless be different from the *status quo*. It will be different for the owner, and it will be different for the customers. (There is a third sort of plan, called an *action plan*, which outlines what precisely will be done when, by whom, and this may accompany a corporate plan.)

Customers

The plan should contain the best available evidence about potential customers. This is not the size of the market; it does not matter how big the market is if the business gets no customers, and some very large markets only have one buyer. The size of the market says nothing about a specific business; stating that 25 million shopping trips are made to a particular location and 'we must be able to succeed because we only want 10,000 customers which is zero point four per cent' means very little. You could argue that if the vast majority of people (99.6%) visiting the area of the proposed location are *not* interested in a particular shop, it is likely to be in the wrong place. Rents in the vicinity will reflect the commercial potential to other retailers of all those non-customers.

Ideally, when potential customers are businesses they should be stated by name, and a promising way of proceeding is to obtain letters of intent from them. Definite orders are better, of course, but this does usually require the customer to be assured that whatever is on order can be delivered. If there is a large or obvious capacity requirement to be completed first (such as a tunnel under the English Channel) there is bound to be something of a provisional nature in any promise. The fact is – and it is *a fact* – that however well-intentioned the promising customer, there is an element of doubt. The entrepreneur must be able to deliver what is promised, and this cannot always be guaranteed, since it is again likely to be a new experience. (In the unusual event that the customer is so keen to obtain something from this new business that cannot be obtained elsewhere, the customer is likely to be able to help, possibly with finance, but also in other respects such as providing premises and equipment.)

Competence

There are two respects in which the authors of a plan need competence, both to do whatever they say they can of a technical (ie physical) nature, and also to take on the responsibilities of creating and maintaining the business which sustains their activities. In this latter respect, a track record of having done so before is a great advantage, particularly if it means that the persons involved are wealthy and successful business customers of their bank manager. In the US it is reckoned that people who have tried and failed before are good bets to know what they are doing next time. This adage receives lip service in the UK, but whether there are investors for whom it is an article of faith, one doubts. Venture capitalists, who specialise in investing in entrepreneurial schemes, still tend to be averse to start-ups. A group of students from Stanford University studying entrepreneurial activity in the UK once concluded speculatively that where Americans strive for success, Britons fear failure.[2]

In the absence of a track record, the authors of a business plan can at least show themselves to be business-like in their approach to preparing their document. It should be apparent that they have prepared their proposal from the perspective of understanding customers, and calculated the financial consequences of their proposed actions. It is for this reason that people should write their own business plans, and why investors should be cautious with people who do not. Over time, I have become convinced that for seasoned lenders, this – and not the forecasts it contains – is the real point of a business plan. Anything can happen after the launch, and one is looking for signs of the people being able to cope when it does. Venture capitalists support this with the adage that 'a first class team with a second class product is better than vice versa', but here I am not so sure. In my research work I was granted confidential access to 7,000 reports prepared on its business customers by a major bank, and in a sample of 10 per cent not once did I find a partnership of more than three founders which had survived intact beyond the first couple of years. They always seemed to fall out. A first class

---

[2] It was not merely the students' own conclusion. In typical enterprising fashion, they went out and asked all sorts of people for their opinions.

team usually contains four or more people – chief executive, plus specialists in production, sales/marketing, finance, etc.

Capacity

The other aspect of competence (to deliver whatever is required in the broadly technical sense) is often related to a capacity issue. A straightforward proposition such as, 'We need to serve 200 customers between noon and 2 pm,' to make a sandwich bar succeed may require a certain amount of practice before it is achievable. Being able to quote surrogate experience might then be useful, such as the proprietor working for a while in a similar establishment. It would also provide an opportunity to count the customers and support the proposal with collateral evidence from a similar set-up. It is a different matter with an investment in a new fully-automated plant to produce say, right-threaded splod-cobblings at a basic cost of 2 ecus each. Before anyone is likely to believe that it can be done (for it is in the nature of new projects to take longer, cost more, and be less productive than planned) much money has to be spent. It is for this reason that innovation on a major scale is usually undertaken by large corporations.

There are many circumstances where the capacity investment simply has to be made before there is any prospect of starting to trade (ie supplying customers). An issue that then arises is how long will it be before the capacity is ready – and further, how long will it be until it reaches utilisation at acceptable levels. Other things being equal, a very big investment will take a longer time, and needs to be financed accordingly. In 1995, the Health Care International project in Clydebank went into receivership within six months of opening. It had been established to attract affluent patients with critical medical conditions from overseas, and it was probably true that people in its identified markets simply did not become seriously ill fast enough to fill the institution so quickly. Despite being 'the largest start-up in Scottish history', the project was under-capitalised. Perhaps it did not look so attractive planned over a longer time perspective. The economics of lobster farming look quite promising when the cost of running the farm is compared to the price of lobsters; the problem is the five years it takes lobsters to reach maturity.

If capacity proves too limited – that is, the new business is inundated with customers – this can also be a problem, as the customers rapidly become dissatisfied and go elsewhere. Raising the price does not always help in this situation, since the price level may be what attracted them in the first place. Despite such uncertainties, there can be some calculations in a business plan which show that the capacity planned is adequate on paper for the forecast sales at the proposed prices. In other words, 'If things happen as we hope, it will work.' The corollary to this is, 'If they don't, we will cope,' and there is a school of thought which holds that 'coping' and 'planning' modes of activity are opposites. Let us hope they are not, for while the most brilliant coper will not succeed if planning is the only way to break the vicious circle, it is no good just sitting there unable to cope with actual events because they were not anticipated in the plan.

Cash

The scale on which a business is planned is one determinant of the cash needed, although there is much that can be done in trying different scenarios (particularly now that spreadsheets are widely available and easy to use) to manipulate the total investment. It is possible – and tempting – to start with a figure which appears to be in some sense 'borrowable' and prepare a forecast which shows that to be the amount required. It is also very silly, for just about the worst thing to do with a business is run out of cash before it has a chance to prove itself – and remember that 'proving itself' for many people means operating profitably.

Starting 'on a small scale' because it requires less capital is essentially flawed, even if it is exceedingly tempting. Even the simplest business will benefit from some efficiencies of scale, and setting up a business which would not be able to compete with a bigger version of itself is asking for trouble. This is particularly true if it is novel, for it will attract imitators who become its competitors. The ideal business start-up comes ready-made with its own barriers to competition.

Whether by accident or design, scale was an issue for the US package delivery business of Federal Express. Several attempts were required before sufficient finance was raised to provide this overnight package delivery service with the necessary scale to operate profitably when it started in the early

1970s.[3] Perhaps this was a good example of 'not taking no for an answer.' It is also a case of 'the exception that proves the rule' – something every bank manager can tell tales about – an outlook without which we would probably not have independent record labels, or boutiques selling socks and lingerie at railway stations'.

It is possible to start a business on a small scale where it is a pilot for an operation which will, for example, have many branches, but the basic trading unit should not be disadvantaged in any way compared to the version that is envisaged operating in the chain. Otherwise, the pilot will not prove much that is useful. In any case, it will be subject to questions of whether its location is typical. The purpose of any pilot or prototype activity should be clear, and its performance measurable against its original objectives. Specifically, it may lack the buying power and/or bear too excessive management costs to operate profitably on its own. Big companies would normally open a chain of stores to start, since pilots merely give advance warning, thus letting competitors plan their response. A chain offers initial scale economies in buying, logistics, etc, and a greater margin for error in that it is affordable if a couple of locations tend to be poor (versus a disaster if it is the only one). The initial experience is also more generalisable.

Commitment

To complete another set of 5Cs[4], the ultimate factor is psychological. Bankers seek collateral security from entrepreneurs because, while they might not doubt the latters' involvement, they do not want them to walk away if the going gets tough. This is one of several necessary characteristics of people starting businesses which are essentially paradoxical in their nature.

---

[3] Federal Express worked on the hub principle, with planes flying in and out of a central sorting facility in Memphis from important cities. In the early phases, there were not enough cities in the network to support the fixed operations of the planes and hub. Adding more cities to the network coverage increased opportunities both for more customers and more traffic from existing customers, but it also required more planes. This increased capacity demanded more revenue to support it, which required more cities in the network, and so on . . . but as we now know, the sequence had a finite limit.

[4] See the 5Cs of the Marketing Mix, Chapter 10.

Too much commitment is called obsession, and obsessed people are not good at listening to what potential customers have to say. On the other hand, they have to believe in themselves and be optimistic; but too much optimism is foolhardiness, surely the last thing needed to launch a business with someone else's money. Also, should they spend the money quickly to create the biggest impact, or eke it out slowly to survive longest? Do you like your entrepreneurs to have a long-term vision of where their enterprise is going in six years' time, or just the determination to see the first six months through? Much research effort has gone into trying to identify the characteristics and norms of successful entrepreneurs. It has resulted in long lists of traits, qualities, characteristics, backgrounds and circumstances, but it is essentially inconclusive. This should not come as a surprise, for – by the fact of what they do – entrepreneurs are not normal.[5]

Corporate venturing – where companies undertake various new business activities – is a fashion which comes and goes (possibly with new generations of managers) in large corporations, but it never seems to last long. In theory, the big corporation can be much more resourceful as a banker than just a plain bank, and 'corporate venturers' do not have to share the attendant concerns independents face in creating and maintaining the infrastructure to employ, and pay, themselves. Still, genuine new businesses – those which are really experimental and speculative in their approach to the market – do not seem to work under large company umbrellas. Perhaps it is the problem of commitment that no one quite has it, or dare show it – to the same extent as the person whose very own creation – and psyche, therefore – is on the line.

WHERE TO NEXT?

Selling is always a barrier for a new venture (Chapter 4)
Service businesses have their own set of issues (Chapter 8)
Working capital needs can be greater than fixed investment (Chapter 14)
There is no substitute for forecasting (Chapter 17)

[5] This is meant literally. The dominant characteristic of entrepreneurs is that they do not conform to social, political, or economic *norms*, and are not, therefore, *normal*. It is not surprising that traditional social science methodology, with its origins in the measurement of normal distributions, fails to come to conclusions about entrepreneurs.

SECTION 4

The financial implications of trading

13. Depreciation and the value of assets

When a business needs assets which will last a long time, it ***sells things for less money than it spends in the short term****.*
Depreciation compensates for the discrepancy

In everyday life, more or less the only time we encounter depreciation is with cars. For most of us, a car is the only asset we expect to sell as it declines in value. The biggest asset most people own is their home, which is often sold, but generally expected to increase in value. Of course, this is not always the case in the short term, as people found after the end of the 1980s boom. It is definitely not true that commercial property will always increase in value, nor that investment in commercial property is guaranteed to be sound (as the developers of Canary Wharf found). Like other things in business, buildings are worth the use they can be put to. A custom-built factory, designed for a business which no longer requires it, is very unlikely to be worth more than it cost to build, since anyone else wanting to use it would have to spend money re-designing it to serve a different purpose. For this and other reasons, it is important not to approach business expenditure with domestic expectations.

As a rule at home, we do not sit down and think about the fact that one day we will need to replace the chair in which we are sitting. It could be that it will fall apart (ie cease to function), or that it will clash with new decor (become obsolete). If we acquire new furniture, this particular chair might be relegated to the spare bedroom or playroom, where it will spend its last years in obscure retirement or go out in a blaze of glory when November 5th comes round.

The fact is, when we buy a chair, mostly we do it on the basis of immediate need, coupled with the knowledge of how much we can afford to spend. This relates to the amount of savings or other spare cash we have, or – more likely when we are younger – how much we can manage to afford monthly for HP or credit card repayments. The institutions who advance us money in this way have ways of imposing limits on overall expenditure; in times of high interest rates, there may sometimes be periods when a fashion for sitting upon home-made bean bags (instead of chairs) becomes very popular.

Personal expenditure is generally linked directly to income. We spend roughly what we can afford – though it takes some people longer than others to learn how to do this. This is an issue well documented in Charles Dickens, showing that it definitely predates the age of plastic money. For most people, how much they can afford these days is determined by how much they and their families are paid at work.

Business expenditure

Having stated that a different perspective is required in business, it is worth risking a little confusion to point out that there are many instances of businesses not doing what, strictly, they should. (This could be because of all the people to be found working in them whose instincts are to follow domestic behaviour.) Examples are marketing and training budgets, which are typically reduced following poor trading performances. Logically, there is every reason that they should be increased, to improve performance. Marketing activity precedes the sales it generates, and training enables people to do things they could not previously do so well or at all. These expenditures should relate to *the income they will generate*, not what has already – and unsuccessfully – passed. It may be good housekeeping to reduce expenditure in response to reduced income, but it is not commonly good business.

Marketing and training are examples of expense items, money which is 'spent' in the course of generating sales, and not money 'invested' in assets – things which a business owns and maintains in order to operate at all. In private life, the distinction is unimportant; it is our prerogative to choose to starve seated in period armchairs, or to eat lobster while reclining on bean bags. 'Investment' is something we may choose to do with any money we are lucky enough not to need to spend. A business, in contrast, must 'invest' the money it is provided with, or it will achieve nothing. It requires assets which will enable it to trade effectively in its chosen sphere. Thus, no matter how good its lobster, a restaurant is unlikely to succeed unless it also invests in chairs for customers to sit upon.

Once again, the great diversity of the business world can come up with exceptions, but these only prove the rule, as the expression goes. Yes, there are businesses for which investment in the financial sense is their actual trade; ignore these. There are also restaurants without chairs, notably in the Wall Street district of New York where there are far too many people for everyone to sit down at street level; these are not restaurants in other than a very functional, obsolete use of the term, and are better called lunch counters. It is not known whether there have ever been restaurants where the customers sat on bean bags – it may have happened in San Francisco at some point in recent history. An American text from the seventies records the story of experimental restaurants where the customers brought and cooked their own food. This concept was 'brainstormed' in response to the criticism that one thing people did not care for about contemporary restaurants was the lack of home-cooked food. There are no prizes for guessing how they fared.

Fixed assets

So, businesses need to own assets, things they will keep which will enable them to trade, such as chairs in restaurants. (For the sake of getting to the point, let us ignore the fact that they can sometimes choose to lease or rent these things.) Owned assets will decline in value as they are used by workers (or customers, in the case of restaurant chairs), but how much they can subsequently be sold for is not a concern. They are expected to remain in use until they are replaced. Such permanent items are not the only assets owned by the business – it could well have money in the bank, and it will probably have things that it does intend to sell. Those it intends to keep are called *fixed assets*. They are 'fixed' in the sense that they are expected to remain within the business. (Before you ask, the chairs in a restaurant do not have to be attached to the floor to qualify; fixed assets can be moved around.)

There are various types of fixed asset:

Land and buildings
Plant and machinery
Office equipment
Fixtures and fittings (a working definition of these is that they *are* attached permanently to floor, wall or ceiling)
Motor vehicles
Other types
Intangible assets, such as patents, licences, trade marks

Additionally, there are differing opinions about the proper accounting treatment of intangibles such as brands, and goodwill (the name sometimes given to the surplus paid over the value of the assets obtained in an acquisition of another company).

It is a basic principle of accounting, and of company law, that a business should be able – and be required – to state the value of its assets. The issue is how should this be determined? Their value may be what they are worth, but the chances are that they will be worth different amounts to different parties. We are familiar with the factors that affect the value of a used motor car – age, physical condition and mileage all come into play – but these are factors which affect its resale, and the whole point of fixed assets is that they are not about to be sold. Their value is therefore determined by what they are worth *to the business that owns them*, according to some guiding principles. One of these is that the company operates a consistent policy towards the valuation of its assets. Another is that of good stewardship, namely that it will take proper care of them. However, the most fundamental is that the business will continue to trade, and so make use of its assets. This is known as the *going concern* principle.

Depreciation

It is clear that a restaurant's chairs will not go on for ever, but it is assumed that the restaurant will. At any point in time, the chairs will be worth somewhere between what they cost originally, and zero. (If they should realise something on disposal when they are replaced, this is an unexpected bonus.)

The management should have an idea of – or at least a policy about – when this replacement will be. A straightforward way of working out interim values is to allocate the original expenditure over the expected life of the asset, as so determined. Thus, if the chairs cost £6,000 and are expected to last five years, their annual reduction in value – or *depreciation charge* – each year will be £1,200 per year. After three years, the chairs will have declined in value by 3 × £1,200 = £3,600 (the *accumulated depreciation*); they will now be worth this much less than their cost, namely £6,000 - £3,600 = £2,400, on the assumption that the business is a going concern. To emphasise this point, this is referred to as the *net book value* of the asset, meaning what it implies: the value shown in the accounting books of the company.

In the majority of cases, this will bear little or no relationship to what the company could obtain for the assets if it tried to sell them. Computer equipment is soon out-dated and worth very little, and complex installations may actually cost money to dispose of. Occasionally, assets which are being depreciated may actually gain in market value, though these are more likely to be 'non-working' things such as works of art, or residential houses.

The type of depreciation in the example above is referred to as *straight line* (named because of the graphical representation of the value plotted against time). The main alternative method is known as *reducing balance*, where the asset's value declines each year by a fixed percentage of its value at the beginning of the year. There are also methods involving *annuity calculations*, and allocations of *units of production*. The annuity method seeks the 'fairest' allocation of the original purchase price over a period of time by allowing for the time-related value of money. The allocation to units of production involves an annual charge being made based upon the use to which the asset is put that year compared to estimates of its total physical life. This method might be used when usage is expected to build up over time, where other methods would unfairly penalise a project in its early stages. Examples are cellular phone and other networks which are poorly utilised when they are developing a customer base. A driving school might choose to depreciate its cars on the basis of the number of lessons given, as this factor would dominate others in the replacement decision. In contrast, a firm of funeral directors might wish to allocate a realistic annual cost to its vehicles, in the knowledge that they will last a long time.

All these methods involve assumptions about the life of the asset, and what determines it. They are potentially subject both to error and abuse. The exception is the reducing balance method, where the annual charge is guaranteed to decline, yet the asset is never fully depreciated, and therefore continues to appear in the firm's accounts. This appearance is useful in drawing attention to the asset, but otherwise, the method appears to have least to do with realism. It is the one used by the Inland Revenue for computing tax allowances against investment in fixed assets.

It is important throughout that the company's policy should be stated, and that it should be consistent. The depreciation charge each year is a deduction in the Profit and Loss account, but it is not actual monetary expenditure. It is better thought of as a 'putting by' of some of the company's income which it would otherwise have declared as profit, to 'repay' the original expenditure for the asset.

The shareholders are obviously interested to know that the management of the company are acting prudently on their behalf, and the provision of adequate depreciation is one such consideration. Such accounting principles originated in the days when inflation was more or less unheard of, and are based therefore on the *historic cost convention*, which means that values are entered into the company's books at the monetary values assigned to them at the time. In periods of inflation, this nominal amount of the original purchase will decline sharply in current value over time. As a result, there have been many contentious circumstances in which property has been revalued in companies' books, with sometimes devastating effect. There is a more obviously defensible issue, along the lines of the argument about marketing and training expenditure, which reasons that the depreciation charge is not – or should not be – a 'repayment' of past expenditure so much as a provision for the future replacement cost of the asset. This became a serious issue in the 1970s in the UK when inflation was rampant, and the concept of current cost accounting (as opposed to historic) was introduced. Fortunately, around the time that the accountancy profession attempted to face up to the prospects of the values of everything in a set of accounts changing every year – effectively meaning that nothing would be 'real' any more – inflation was brought under control, and replacement cost accounting was generally shelved.

Current assets

Only fixed assets are depreciated. To a supplier of restaurant furniture, chairs are items awaiting sale, and are classified as *stock* (in the US, *inventory*). The pedants amongst us will note that the office chairs in this new company are of course fixed assets, and if they should have a staff restaurant, the chairs . . . etc. The point to remember is that the usage determines the classification. Stocks are a class of *current assets*, a term which, like many used in accounting, does not mean quite what appears. Current does not mean so much 'just there at the moment' as 'flowing through' the firm. In fact, the furniture showroom will very much want its stock of chairs to 'flow out' to customers, but it will also then replace them. Clearly, the going concern principle applies to stock. When it is sold, the firm will want to sell it for more than its value, as this is the fundamental basis of profit, but its worth in the books is only fairly stated provided it remains saleable. For this reason, stock is valued at *the lower of cost and realisable value*.

The other types of current assets are *cash* – which may be in tills and safes, but is probably in banks (the accounting term is confusing[1]) – and *debtors*, who are people (businesses probably) who owe money to the company. The value of cash is not normally subject to going concern considerations (unless the company in question is a bank perhaps) but debtors are, since if the business ceases to trade, the incentive for them to settle their accounts declines sharply. In full, the debtors category includes all monies owed to the firm in the short term. As well as customers who have bought on account, this covers sums paid in advance for services and facilities, such as rent. These are called *prepayments*, and of course, very much assume that the business is a going concern.

---

[1] Currency is usually known as *petty cash*, when it is kept by the business for the purposes of settling small local transactions and reimbursing expenses. When currency is in the tills or cash registers of the business, it is known as *cash in hand*. A *cash business* is one which does not extend credit terms to its customers, but they might well pay by cheque or Switch.

Business finance

So, what basically happens with money in a business is this:

- Shareholders give money to the business to enable it to trade. They cannot have this back, but under the principle of limited liability, they cannot be made to cough up any more whatever happens (an important principle in attracting them in the first place). In return for this money, they 'own' part of the business.

- They do not own a physically identifiable part, nor a part of everything the business owns. The business is a separate legal person (entity).

- The business spends some or all of the money:
  On fixed assets, from which to trade
  On stock, which it may buy or make, with which to trade
  On expenses, incurred in the process of trading

- It then generates revenue, from the sales it makes.

- For reasons of convenience, efficiency and security, most business transactions are for credit, and money changes hands at different times from goods.

- This means that the customers of the business may owe it money (they are debtors), and the business itself may owe money to its suppliers (known as creditors).

Periodically, the business is called upon to explain to shareholders what has happened to their money, so it maintains accounts. At the appointed time, the balances of each of these accounts are summarised, in a document called a Balance Sheet, as follows:

Extracts from Marks & Spencer plc Balance Sheet as at 31 March 1997

	(£ million)	
Fixed Assets*		
Land and buildings	3057	
Fixtures, fittings and equipment	500	
Other	90	
		3647
Current assets*		
Stocks	445	
Debtors	1726	
Investments	361	
Cash at bank and in hand	672	
		3204
Current liabilities*		
Creditors: amounts falling due in less than one year	1775	
Net current assets**		1429
Total assets less current liabilities**		5076
Creditors: amounts falling due after more than one year	528	
Net assets**		4548
Share capital and reserves	1444	
Profit and loss account	3104	
Total capital employed**		4548

*Note that items marked * are category headings, and items marked ** are totals, sub-totals or differences obtained from the entries.*

Double-entry bookkeeping

The total assets of the business less the creditors are known as the *net assets* (very much on the going concern principle, what the business has left after allowance for what it owes to others). If the net assets are more than the money the shareholders provided in the first place, the business has obviously 'made money' – it has made a profit. Conversely, if the net assets are less, then it has made a loss. Obviously, this profit or loss will equal the difference between the revenues from customers and the expenses incurred (not necessarily the same as the payments made). Listing and cross-checking all the transactions which are the result of trade is the process of balancing the books, which is perfectly simple to do in theory – and notoriously difficult to achieve in practice.

The specialised – and in some eyes, tedious – process of bookkeeping and the preparation of accounts is too arcane for this book, and while there are good reasons for having reliable processes, trial balance and its relatives are not exactly constructive activities compared to other methods of controlling what is happening. Their origins lie in the separation of ownership from control of a business and the need to oversee the actions of the managers, using an independent, professional auditor. There is one fundamental point to be made here which tends to mystify people when they first encounter it – the apparently peculiar practice of writing everything down twice. In fact, it is a perfectly sensible and logical thing to do, as the following demonstration shows:

Imagine that you have just prepared a draft balance sheet for your business when a last minute 'delivery' arrives, and you decide to incorporate its content on to the balance sheet. The 'delivery' could be goods, a letter containing a cheque or demand, an order etc. There will always be at least two changes to make, for example:

The 'delivery'	**Effect on balance sheet**
A delivery of stock, with invoice	Increase Stocks (with the value) *also* Increase Creditors (with the invoice)

A delivery of stock, COD; You pay the messenger	Increase Stocks, as above *also* Decrease Cash with the payment
A cheque in settlement of a customer's bill	Decrease Debtors by the amount *also* Increase Cash*
A final demand from a creditor; You post a cheque	Decrease Creditors *also* Decrease Cash*
An order from a customer	Increase Debtors by the amount of the sale *also*
You dispatch the goods and an invoice	Decrease Stocks by the cost of the goods and *also* Increase Profits by the difference!

** The company's cash at bank is determined from the point at which it issues instructions, not when they arrive at the bank.*

It is not for nothing that the Balance Sheet is so named. It lists the balances on the company's books, and – of course – it balances. Nothing listed above has resulted in any duplication. Each entry has a specific purpose, to change one of the values in the books. After each event, the balance sheet continues to balance.

WHERE TO NEXT?

Brands are assets in some people's view (Chapter 2)
Depreciation is a fixed cost (Chapter 7)
Investments in working assets are strategic as well as financial (Chapter 11)
Competitors' investments are good research data (Chapter 18)

14. Working capital

When exactly ***money is spent*** *affects how much a business needs if it is always to be able to pay the bills*

If you owned shares in W H Smith, would the time of day at which the accounts were prepared concern you? Most people take for granted when they go to bed at night that there will be newspapers in the morning – possibly pushed through their letter-boxes – carrying the very news seen on last night's TV. The days when stories 'broke' overnight and thus appeared first in newspapers are long gone. Papers contain much of a magazine or commentary nature, yet it remains a fact that nobody wants to buy yesterday's newspapers. Newspapers become worthless overnight – and W H Smith handles an awful lot of newspapers (it is a major wholesaler as well as a retailer). When do they show in the accounts?

The business of an individual newsagent may not be very big (though there are several large chains besides W H Smith), and the rounds belonging to a single shop are very significant to its business, since the agent can be confident of selling the papers which are delivered daily. There is another financial consideration, that of collecting the money, but the sales are more or less guaranteed, and predictable. Would the same apply if every customer were obliged to visit the shop? Purchasing patterns would be unlikely to follow the 'daily daily' routine, simply because of the extra factors which would get in the way, so the delivery principle is also very important to the publishers who require circulation figures to command advertising revenue as well as that from the cover price. Broadly speaking, with the core sales underwritten in this way, the distributors can afford to encourage the retailers to maintain extra stocks for those people who pop in, have occasional needs, are attracted to a headline, etc. Also, these are the people whom the circulation managers would love to recruit. How else do you get anyone to change papers?

Stocks

The problem for the newsagent is whether there is any money to be made. Suppose the agent can buy the papers at 70% of their cover price, that is, an order for 400 papers priced at 50p will cost £140. Assume also that there is only one title – a fairly common occurrence with evening papers in most areas. The profit per paper is 50p – 35p = 15p. (It may seem pedantic, but it is worth stating that the newsagent cannot buy a single paper for 35p – the average cost figure is only available for bulk purchases.)

When the newsagent has sold 250 papers, he should have a profit of 250 × 15p = £37.50. The cash position is as follows, however:

Paid out for papers	400 × 35p = £140	
Received from sales	250 × 50p = £125	
Cash position		£15 down

This appears to bear no relation to the reported profit of £37.50, but the issue of the remaining papers has yet to be taken into account. The accounting treatment of the situation would be to value the papers *at the lower of cost or realisable value*, and the 'balance sheet' approach to the transaction would read:

Papers in stock at cost	150 × 35p = £52.50
Cash received from customers	250 × 50p = £125.00
Less amount spent on paper stock	400 × 35p = £140.00
Profit	£37.50

It is not difficult to see that this profit is based on the valuation of newspapers at cost. When the end of the day is reached, those daily papers in stock become more or less worthless, the profit is wiped out, and the newsagent has lost £15 on the day's transactions.

If this happened regularly, the response of the newsagent would be to stock fewer shop copies, thus forever restricting the potential circulation of that title. The situation becomes more complex and critical for an individual title when the stock of 400 actually means 20 copies each of 20 titles, and it is for this reason that the newsagent is allowed to buy a proportion of stock on a sale-or-return (SOR) basis. Unsold papers may be returned the following day and their cost 'refunded'.

For the purpose of this chapter, the principle of sale-or-return is intended to be *the exception which demonstrates the rule.* SOR is uncommon; when businesses sell things, generally *they want them to stay sold.* Imagine the confusion that would arise if your local supermarket returned the unsold goods to its suppliers at the end of every day. Most things that sell regularly do not present a problem. A typical newsagent can be confident that his stock of chocolate bars will continue to sell, so the profit on each one can be calculated on the assumption that the stock remaining retains its value. A different approach is needed with Easter Eggs; it is not likely that they can be sold at full price after Easter, but the manufacturers and wholesalers do not want them back. Because of the risk to retailers, Easter Eggs and other date-specific stock items usually carry a bigger margin than standard produce. A few things can actually appreciate in stock, vintage wine perhaps, but most have some finite point at which they deteriorate and/or lose their customer appeal. The original purpose of clearance sales was to convert the season's unsold stock into cash to pay for the new range.

Payment

If sale-or-return solves for the newsagent the problem of newspaper stocks (and it does not apply across the board – there are many magazines on which it is not available, for example), there is still another financial issue to confront which makes running a newsagent's a less straightforward business than might be expected. The corollary of being able to depend on guaranteed daily sales of papers through the delivery rounds is that it is necessary to collect the money. In the days when people were paid weekly, it was very important to do this every week. If customers were once allowed to miss a payment, it became very difficult for them to catch up. Most people paid in cash, much of it coin, and someone had to go and collect it. Nowadays, it is more common for customers to pay monthly, by cheque, and to visit the shop to pay. This still involves the newsagent in sending out bills, and is not without problems. Some newsagents claim that there is no finer moment than when a pompous, irate customer is told that they received no paper that morning because their account was overdue.

The newsagents weekly bill for a typical family can easily be £6–£7, or £25 monthly, so if the shop has rounds totalling 800 homes, by the end of the month, the outstanding bills are worth £20,000. Fortunately, the wholesalers are aware of this, and to some extent the debt will be offset by their credit terms. Traditionally, the agent was required to settle bills weekly. Latterly, it is possible to obtain a month's credit to match that extended to customers, although transactions are still calculated and settled a week at a time. Smaller retailers are less likely to be able to negotiate for monthly credit, so they could find themselves having to provide for three weeks' trade, for which they need either to possess or borrow finance. Even when the terms match, the suppliers are only advancing the cost price, whereas the customers owe the sales value. The profit has still to be collected.

Part of the reason for trade credit is that it is impractical and unwise to attempt to settle every transaction on a cash-on-delivery basis. Financial and physical transactions take place at different times, with delivery notes and other pieces of paper forming the link between them. The normal convention is that the title to goods changes hands when the customer accepts delivery, and the sale is deemed to have been made at that point, even though the invoice may not be received or indeed, issued until later. The availability of supplier credit as a norm varies from sector to sector. Traditional independent booksellers are used to receiving extended credit without which they would be unlikely to stock publishers' books. On the other hand, petrol is supplied to retailers on very low margins, and as deliveries are made for 'cash' – the retailer signs a direct debit – the owner of the station has to pay for the stock of petrol unseen in the tanks before it is sold. It is not surprising that the old tradition where local garage customers were sent monthly accounts has died out. The manner in which credit is dispensed down the distribution channels of different industries varies considerably, from the almost charitable to the pay-up-or-else attitude.

Working capital

The narrow definition of working capital is *the finance required to support the trading activities*. A business will hold *stocks* of goods for sale, and have customers who have bought but not yet paid, who are known as *debtors*. (The American term is *accounts receivable*, which may seem a little pompous but is certainly unambiguous. If in doubt about debtors and creditors, remember it is debtors who go to prison.) The business may not yet have paid for its stock, and so it may therefore owe money to *creditors* (US *accounts payable*). These items are formally entered in the notes to published accounts as *trade debtors* and *trade creditors*, strictly to identify needs arising as a direct consequence of trade.

Reality is, as usual, complicated and a little messy. In addition to trade amounts, there are creditors associated with the routine supply of services which enable a business to operate, such as utilities, and there will be some items where the cost has been incurred but the invoice not received, known as *accruals* or *accrued charges*. Similarly, the business may have paid for things in advance of using them, which gives rise to an item equivalent to debtors, known as *prepayments*. The harmless telephone bill is complicated in accounting terms, carrying as it does amounts for call charges in arrears but rental in advance. At any moment, a business is likely to have made telephone calls which have yet to be billed, giving rise to accrued charges. Meanwhile, it will also have paid rental for a period in the future, which is a prepayment. If a phone bill has arrived and is entered in the books but not yet paid, the telephone company is also a creditor.

These non-trade charges tend to reduce in proportionate significance the bigger a business is, where the financing of trade is predominant.

Manufacturing companies

So far, we have discussed trading companies which buy in goods and sell them on. Businesses which *make things* face more complicated issues in valuing stocks (something they must do for the Inland Revenue whether they need to or not otherwise). Stocks are classified either as *finished goods* (things which have been made and are ready for sale), or *raw materials* (things which have been purchased or otherwise obtained but have yet to be processed; they do not literally have to be raw). There is also something in between, called *work in progress*

(WIP). In practical terms, WIP may have a realisable value, or it may not. A suit of clothes deemed half-finished might actually be a pair of trousers or a jacket and so be worth something; a half-finished parachute would be worth nothing, except a possible suit for negligence if it were accidentally sold.

The principle of the *going concern* – the assumption that the business will be able to continue its trade – is of great importance in the valuation of work in progress where costs associated with work done to raw materials or components are added to its value as it moves through a factory. These costs include overheads associated with the manufacture as well as the labour of the people working on it. The assumption is that 'it' will eventually be finished and sold.

There is potentially a big difference in the working capital requirements of firms which make things for stock and those which make to order. The latter receives an order from a customer which will normally have a delivery date associated with it. The customer may expect credit (this is where the terms *creditor* and *debtor* are confusing – a debtor is given credit, a creditor gives it) but competent management should be able to work out when to make and deliver the order to minimise the need for financing stock, and organise any purchases to make the best use of supplier terms available. A company making for stock is much more likely to be acting speculatively, being less certain when it will sell the items it manufactures, if at all. If the item in question is new – in the sense of an innovation – its 'total cost' may involve 'research & development' and engineering set-up. It is at this stage that questions of 'the lower of cost and realisable value' become complex. The initial cost of a new product may be more than it will be sold for, if its price is determined by expectations of how many will eventually be sold at a greater volume and therefore a different cost. In the made-to-order case, the certainty is much greater, and a common method of fixing a price is to estimate the cost and add a percentage for overheads and profit. This is called *cost-plus pricing*.

Managing working capital

Industries tend to have norms, standards or expectations of credit terms and payments. In big firms, bills are processed through automated systems; 'cheque runs or BACS batches' – when the central computer is loaded with cheque paper and facsimile signatures, or connected to another machine in the bank – take place on specific days only, partly for reasons of security. Learning when to send invoices to regular customers so that they arrive just before and not after the deadline for an automated system run can be worth a month's credit. Firms normally issue *statements* as well as invoices, summarising all items due for payment and noting anything overdue. Some choose to pay items 'on statement' rather than against individual invoices, perhaps on grounds of efficiency. The question of whose terms dominate whom tends to be a function of where the power lies in the distribution chain. The ultimate sanction for non-payment is the withholding of future orders, but a supplier will obviously be reluctant to do this if it means risking the loss of the customer's future business. Small firms are widely said to suffer at the hands of big ones, but there are plenty of stories of frenetic small-firm owners creating such a fuss that the more relaxed big company staff are willing to make a special effort for the sake of an easy life.

Good working capital management has helped the growth of supermarket chains. While the poor independent grocer has to go to the aptly named cash-and-carry wholesaler, the bulk buyer trades directly with manufacturers, obtaining credit for goods which are sold for cash before they have to be paid for. Tesco's accounts for the year ended 22 February 1997 show stocks of £490 million and trade creditors of £826 million. Allowing for the fact that the latter includes an element representing VAT while the former is net of VAT, it is clear that Tesco has sold around £250–300 million's worth of goods and not yet paid the suppliers. Who would dare withhold a delivery until the account was settled? At the corresponding date in 1996, stock was £461 million, and trade creditors £764 million, so trade creditors have increased faster than the change in stock. Marks & Spencer's accounts to 31 March 1997 show stocks of £445 million and trade creditors of £223 million, so M & S had paid for about half their stock. Storehouse (owners of Bhs, Mothercare, and Children's World) show stocks of £175 million at 29 March 1997, and trade creditors of £63 million, perhaps a reflection of the slower-moving range of goods sold by Storehouse.

Ratios

Working capital needs for given levels of trade can be calculated from norms, and comparisons made of how firms manage their individual needs. This involves calculating fairly crude but nevertheless useful ratios where the expressions 'days' or 'turn' are used. 'Days' are literally the average number of days it takes for debtors to pay and creditors to be paid. 'Turn' is used for stocks, to express the number of times that stock is replaced within an accounting year. There is an assumption of homogeneity about the stock – and therefore, some uncertainty when businesses are expanding or contracting rapidly – but basically, the value of stocks at cost (STOCKS) is compared to the *cost of goods sold* (COGS) for the year. COGS for the year divided by STOCKS gives a figure usually expressed to the nearest whole number which is said to be the number of times stock 'turns over' during the year. Alternatively, the expression (STOCKS × 365) ÷ COGS compares the current level with the previous year's consumption and computes how many days it will last.

The creditors total can be used similarly to work out how many days – strictly on average – the firm takes to pay its suppliers. This involves the trade creditors (TC) and PURCHASES, goods bought for resale during the year (not necessarily the same thing as COGS, and certainly not the same for a manufacturing company.[1]) The expression (TC × 365) ÷ PURCHASES gives an approximation. TC includes VAT and PURCHASES does not, so a final adjustment is needed. The same adjustment is applied to debtor days where the denominator of the expression is sales, or turnover. This calculation of 'days' is only properly meaningful if all customers are on the same terms.

The supposition above of slower moving stock at Storehouse can be tested (see over):

---

[1] The accountants' use of the word 'purchases' is strictly limited. Copier paper may be purchased, but it is not included in purchases.

From the 1997 accounts

	Stock	COGS	Trade Creditors	Purchases
		(£ million)		
Storehouse	175	835	63	886
Marks & Spencer	445	5104	223	5126
Tesco	490	11151	826	11180

(Some of these figures have to be part-calculated, part-estimated from the published figures. Although the idea of publishing accounts might be thought of as encouraging the purchase of their shares, the objective for many companies seems to be to reveal as little information as possible.)

The accompanying ratio calculations are:

	Stockturn	Stock in days	Creditor days
Storehouse	4.8	65	26
Marks & Spencer	11.5	27	16
Tesco	22.8	16	27

The assumption with stock days is that only Tesco trades on Sundays, and therefore the other two have 6-day weeks. Creditor days are calculated on a 7-day week, because that is how long suppliers wait for payment.

These ratios show that the proportional differences between Tesco and Storehouse is not to do with the length of credit they demand. Both take about a month to pay, which sounds reasonable. The difference between the stores is the amount of time goods take to sell. The nature of the goods sold in the shops is reflected in the stockturns, but M & S is something of a hybrid, as 43 per cent of sales were of food, which turns over extremely quickly, and the remainder were of clothing, home furnishings, etc. Marks & Spencer appear to pay more promptly, and one can only speculate why, for the accounts do not reveal the reasons. One possibility is that the averaging of total figures disguises the fact that non-food terms are around the 27 days of its competitors, but that the company pays very promptly for the very fresh food it sells. To test this, one could go back over time and see how creditor days varied with changes in the product mix, but the conclusion would at best be weak, as there are many other possible factors.

Overtrading

Sensible businesses make special efforts to improve the appearance of their published accounts by running down stocks and collecting debtors as the accounting reference date (the official name for the financial year end) approaches. In general, the usefulness of ratios is also limited by the range of different business activities to be found within a single set of accounts. However, for businesses in broadly one sector, inter-company comparisons – and trends over time – can reveal interesting insights.

For the people running the businesses of course, all necessary data should be available to maintain useful operating benchmarks. Managing working capital effectively can make a big difference to overall capital needs. Businesses which start on a shoestring can suffer from a phenomenon banks refer to as *overtrading*, meaning that they are unable to finance their working capital needs internally, and thus look to their bankers to lend them the necessary. The bank takes the view that this is too risky, and that their lending should be matched by capital within the firm. This can be very frustrating to the entrepreneurs, who see the banks as denying them the opportunity of growing to generate the very profits which would result in improvements to their capital base! Banks observe that the absence of a capital base implies a lack of profitability, and with it a probability that increases in trading activity are at the expense of both profit margins and prompt settlement. The firm is working very hard for very little, and is very risky.

There is validity in both sides of this debate and, in fact, there are alternative methods available for financing genuine working capital needs such as factoring and invoice discounting. Where there is no dispute is when the term 'working capital' is used to mean unrecoverable operating costs which must be incurred before any trade can be generated at all. Lending banks are not interested in this; they like to finance assets, not to discharge liabilities. They take the view that the owners of the business need to provide this kind of capital themselves. If the business proposition is sufficiently attractive, business angels or venture capitalists who invest directly in businesses may be interested, subject to the risks and potential returns involved.

WHERE TO NEXT?

Promotional events affect stock holdings (Chapter 3)
As do delivery terms (Chapter 6)
Distribution channels can set their own credit terms (Chapter 10)
Forecasting helps to anticipate working capital needs (Chapter 17)

15. Gearing – the use of borrowed capital

Businesses ***spend money*** *before they earn it, and there is a choice of whether to obtain it permanently, or borrow for a period*

Gearing is the British word for what Americans call leverage, and both terms refer to the use of borrowed money in the capital base of a business. 'Leveraging' came to the UK in a big way in the mid-1980s when LBOs and LBIs – leveraged buy-outs and buy-ins – became the fashion, typically of business units no longer required by their parent companies. You can use either word; 'gearing' may sound a little old-fashioned in some circles – and remember to pronounce the other word like 'beverage'.

Both words describe the properties of simple machines. *Leverage* magnifies the effect of a force, and *gears* are used to vary the relationship between the speed of an engine and the wheels carrying it. In a business, the investors' capital (shareholders' funds) can be geared up – or leveraged – to greater effect by borrowing money to work alongside it in the business. Under skilful management, this can be a highly effective strategy, but when things go wrong, running a highly geared business can feel like riding a highly geared bicycle uphill – very hard work, and extremely difficult to get going again if it comes to a halt.

Gearing ratio

The *gearing ratio* of a business is the proportion of its capital base which is borrowed money and has therefore at some stage to be repaid to the lender, unlike the shareholders' funds which are expected to remain permanently invested. (Individual shareholders may sell their shares, of course, if there is a market for them, but this does not alter the underlying investment.)

There are two ways of expressing the gearing ratio, with the *borrowed capital* computed as a percentage of either the *total capital*, or of the *shareholders' funds* (also known as *equity*). Both are valid; the important thing, as with the margin and mark-up percentages,[1] is to know which you are talking about. A business with a capital base of £10 million, of which £3 million is borrowed, could be said to have a gearing ratio of 3 divided by 10, or 30%. Alternatively, as the equity in the firm must be £7 million (being total capital of 10 minus 3 million borrowings), the ratio could be expressed as three-sevenths or roughly 43%.

If you hear of a 100% ratio, it is almost certainly not a business in which all the capital is borrowed, so it will mean that the equity and borrowings (also referred to as *debt* in this context) are equal. Gearing ratios of over 100% clearly indicate businesses in which the majority of capital is borrowed. Beware of a 50% ratio; it could mean that the debt is 50% of the equity, or that it is 50% of the capital, and so 100% of the equity.

High street bankers lending money to small businesses often talk of a fifty-fifty debt-equity split. They also call this 'one-for-one-lending', meaning that they will lend the business one pound for each pound the owners invest personally. Although they will deny this if you ask – insisting that each case is treated on its merits – many bank managers use *one-for-one* as a rule of thumb to limit the level of risk they are willing to contemplate, for it is the *level of risk* which gearing affects.

The risk of gearing

Apart from this somewhat arbitrary 50:50 figure, there is no particular value which a gearing ratio should or should not assume. The primary purpose of all financial ratios is to make comparisons possible, in order to show the differences between comparable companies, and to demonstrate trends over time. To understand the effects of gearing, we are going to have to look at examples and perform some simple arithmetic.

There are two consequences of using borrowed money to fund a business – you have to pay a charge for its use, known as *interest*, and you have, at some point, to *repay* the money to the lender. To emphasise this distinction, imagine you were hiring

---

[1] See page 56.

a van instead of money. You would have to pay a rental charge for the use of the vehicle, and this would be a business expense, chargeable to the Profit and Loss account. Eventually, you would return the vehicle to its rightful owner, and this would have no direct effect on the P & L, although it might affect your capacity to do certain things in the future. When the 'vehicle' rented is actually money, the same situation applies – interest is charged to the P & L account, but repayments are not. The difference is that as the whole point of borrowing money is to spend it, having to manage events so that money is available when repayments are due is an added responsibility and constraint.

To observe the effects of gearing, consider the examples of two businesses whose actual trading patterns are identical. WEE (Wholly Equity Enterprise) is financed by £3 million of shareholders' funds; BIG (Business Including Gearing) has £1 million equity, and a £2 million loan, on which it pays 10% per annum interest.

	WEE	**BIG**
(Figures in £000s)		
Sales	5000	5000
Cost of sales	(3000)	(3000)
Gross profit	2000	2000
Overheads	(1100)	(1100)
Profit before interest & tax (PBIT)	900	900
Interest	–	(200)
Tax	(270)	(210)
Net profit after tax	630	490

(The rate of tax is assumed to be 30%. Interest is tax deductible, so the taxable profit of BIG is 900 – 200 = 700.)

So what is the big deal? WEE, the business without borrowings, makes more profit overall, but the shareholders have invested more money in it. To compare the two, we need to consider the *level of return* they obtain on their respective investments. This is a suitable point to introduce two more ratios. *The Return on Capital Employed* (ROCE) of a business is defined as the *Profit Before Interest & Tax* divided by the *Capital Employed* (equal to the total invested, and therefore the net assets of the business). It measures the general ability of the management to invest whatever capital they have in suitable assets to generate profits. In this case, as we gave WEE and BIG identical trading patterns, they naturally have identical ROCEs of 900/3000. Normally, this would be expressed as a percentage, in this case 30%.

The Return on Shareholders' Funds (ROSF) – also known as *Return on Equity* (ROE) – shows the position after the borrowings etc have been accounted for, and is defined as *Net Profit After Tax* divided by *Shareholders' Funds*. For WEE, this is 630/3000, that is 21%; for BIG it is 490/1000, that is 49%!

So, the shareholders of BIG get a much better return on their money than the owners of WEE. However, we have to establish exactly what 'return' means in this scenario.

The steady state

If the businesses have no need of further capital WEE would be free to distribute to its shareholders its net profits of £630,000, or 21 pence per £1 share. (In reality, this almost never happens.) BIG would not be able to pay all its net profits (£490,000) though, because it would have to make provision first for repaying the loan. It is likely that some, but not all, of the cash needed for this would be provided through the *depreciation charge*. So, suppose that BIG has to fund repayments of £200,000 per annum from its profits; this still leaves £290,000, which could be paid to shareholders at the rate of a 29 pence dividend per £1 share.

This is the basic attraction of gearing – the shareholders get *more* for their money! It is not difficult to see that this is because the lenders are prepared to accept a lower 'earnings' rate, provided they also get their money back. If there continued to be no reinvestment, eventually BIG would have paid off its loan, by which time its shareholders' funds would have reached the same level as WEE's. (The accounting procedures through which this happens are complicated, but basically, if the two companies have identical assets and neither has any debts, they must have the matching equity.[2]) Consequently, BIG's shareholders would have a non-realised capital gain, as each £1 share would be backed by £3 of assets. Their rate of dividend would have declined to that of WEE's. On the other hand, WEE's shareholders would have received much larger payments in total during the intervening years. Which is better? Well, to some extent, it is a case of taking the choice and paying the money!

Growth scenarios

When businesses are trading in fairly stable conditions and are not expected to demonstrate fast growth, high gearing has considerable attractions, particularly as a means of eventually transferring ownership, and it was this that made LBOs attractive. It was only after the new owners started floating the businesses on the stock market and quickly paying off the debt that bankers woke up to the risk-return profiles they were allowing people to obtain, whereupon terms started to be much less generous for potential new owners. Generally speaking though, investors in shares,[3] and certainly entrepreneurs out to build empires, are more interested in business growth than in making fast bucks.

Growth in individual shares on stock markets often comes about through acquisition and merger, but real, economic, growth derives from the reinvestment of profits into more assets which in turn generate more profits for reinvestment. If our two businesses are seeking to grow in this way, then they will not want to distribute profits to their shareholders. WEE will be able to reinvest 630,000, thus increasing its capital base by 630/3000, that is 21%. In contrast, BIG will first *reduce* its capital base through the loan repayment of 200,000, and then reinvest profits

---

[2] Sticklers for accuracy will point out that this case will actually arise only of there is no depreciation charge – but there is no time for an accountancy class here.

[3] The majority of investments in shares are made by insurance and pension companies who are interested in long-term growth, not short-term gains from dealing in price fluctuations.

of 290,000. This gives a net increase of only 90,000, or 3% of the capital base. It is fairly obvious that gearing is a major barrier to growth. Almost immediately, the businesses cease to be identical in other respects. WEE has the opportunity to grow much quicker than BIG does, and with growth comes the potential for scale economies which alter trading conditions, in favour of WEE.

Partly for this reason, very big companies do not organise borrowings on the 'regular repayment plan' implied here, but smaller ones do, because their bankers are not usually willing to wait several years to get all their money back, even when they hold collateral security. In very small firms, the availability of owners' collateral, often their homes, can influence lending decisions to produce apparently very high gearing ratios, and consequently high ROSF ratios. This happens frequently with independent retail and catering businesses which are bought and sold on commercial mortgages. The owners appear to make high percentage returns, not because their total net profits are high, but because of the low level of equity invested in the business. In practice, such people are really working hard for the finance company.

The willingness of banks to finance growth depends to some extent on the nature of the investment to be made. If funds are required for equipment, for example, then the depreciation charge over its expected life should match the loan repayments. As the depreciation is a set-aside of profits to cover the decline in the value of the asset, cash will be available to meet the loan repayments. There will still be interest charges, but the project may be feasible using debt, and if the associated equipment has a reliable second hand value, specialist finance such as hire purchase may be obtainable. For growth though, additional finance is often needed to provide physical accommodation, and increases in working capital, such as stock and debtors (money owed by customers) in which case the cash repayments will not be covered by the depreciation charge. Banks do not like these situations, and refer to businesses involved therein as 'overtrading'.

Finally, growth usually involves spending money in the beginning to get it back at a later date. However well-planned the former may be, it is essentially speculative, and there is no automatic guarantee of the latter following on. Indeed, the ever present tension in business between maintaining the *status quo*, and pursuing rapid growth makes the future doubly uncertain – the firm's growth strategy may distract its management from the existing business, or even alienate its existing customers. Consequently, smaller businesses pursuing high growth strategies need lots of equity finance, and this is usually provided by institutions known as *Venture Capitalists* or *Equity Partners*, who are not (or at least, say they are not) so bothered about losing the odd investment that goes wrong, so much as 'cleaning up' when the good one really takes off.

The problem of uncertainty

It is the fact that the future cannot be predicted, even in the so-called steady state, that makes gearing an aptly-named concept, with its connotations of a small movement in one place producing a larger one elsewhere. To see this at work, let's look at what happens to WEE and BIG as trading conditions change.

Consider first a general economic downturn:

Sales decline by 10%; margins remain constant at 40%; overheads are unchanged:

	WEE	**BIG**	**BIG**
(£000s)			
Interest rate	–	10%	15%
Sales	4500	4500	
Cost of sales	(2700)	(2700)	
Gross profit	1800	1800	
Overheads	(1100)	(1100)	
Profit before interest & tax	700	700	700
Interest	–	(200)	(300)
Tax	(210)	(150)	(120)
Net profit after tax	490	350	280

Using the measure calculated before, and hereby called 'pence per share available for distribution and/or reinvestment' (this is not actually a 'standard' expression, but it makes the point nicely), WEE is down to 490/3000, that is 16.3 pence per share; BIG however, first has to find the 200,000 loan repayment. This leaves only 150,000 available for shareholders, which works out at 15 pence per share, now less than WEE is achieving.

To allow for another variable, the extra column shows the position if interest rates also rise to 15% (an event which could in fact trigger the economic downturn). After allowance for the repayment, BIG now has only 8 pence per share available for distribution. If conditions continue to decline, its managers will soon be working for the banks.

Of course, in an upturn, things are quite different. You might like to work out for yourself what happens, assuming that the companies can handle extra trade without increasing their overheads. Basically, BIG's shareholders laugh all the way to the bank. The bankers, meanwhile, remain content with their lending policy, which they would regard as earning a safe, reasonable return with their depositors' money.

Now consider a price war instigated by WEE, which BIG has to follow:

Sales return to their original level of volume, but there is a 10% cut in price which lowers the revenue, without a corresponding reduction in the Cost of Sales –

	WEE	**BIG**
(£000s)		
Sales	4500	4500
Cost of sales	(3000)	(3000)
Gross profit	1500	1500
Overheads	(1100)	(1100)
Profit before interest & tax	400	400

Interest	–	(200)
Tax	(120)	(60)
Net profit after tax	280	140

Basically, if WEE's shareholders will accept a drop in earnings for a while, they should be rewarded handsomely fairly soon. BIG is still generating profits, but it is now unable to meet its loan repayments. If the bank forecloses on the loan – and its ability to do this would depend on the terms of the loan agreement; its willingness to do so on the disposable value of the assets forming the security – BIG will probably have to cease trading, leaving the market to WEE, at least until another competitor comes along.

To meet the loan, BIG will have to reduce its costs or sell some of its assets, either of which makes it smaller. To survive at its current size, it needs to generate more revenue. It cannot do so by raising prices. The alternative is to lower them to win some of WEE's customers, or to expand. Lowering prices makes the situation worse, because WEE can 'afford' to match any cuts BIG may make; if BIG is to expand, it needs more capital. Borrowing more will of course increase the gearing and definitely make the situation worse before it has a chance to get better.

This is a very simplistic example, but it is quite possible for real businesses to cease trading when they are profitable, because of the level of gearing. Sometimes, the alternative is for the owners to raise additional equity, but that often means losing control, which can actually turn out to be a worse experience than going out of business. The conundrum is, it is clearly inefficient to run a business with one hundred per cent equity. It will almost certainly need different amounts of funds at different times, and equity – by taking risks – can earn higher rates than banks charge, so opportunities are being wasted if it is idle. The problem is, how much to borrow?

As ever, there is no perfect answer to this question, it is a matter of judging the circumstances. For very large companies. the market system will usually give strong signals if it thinks a company's gearing is getting too high. Yet everything has a price within a market system, and the world's largest takeover to date was effectively a leveraged buy-in. Small businesses are said to fail because of a lack of *adequate capital*, yet they invariably start with all the capital they can raise, so if that is consistently inadequate, this market also appears to be imperfect. Most new businesses do not succeed, yet, whatever the publicity may say, banks rarely have serious bad debt problems from business lending – but perhaps this is because of their insistence on collateral security rather than their ability to fine-tune gearing ratios. A few exceedingly successful businesses were started under the Loan Guarantee Scheme of the 1980s (through which the government encouraged banks to make loans which they would not otherwise have considered, using a higher interest rate to provide the 'guarantee'), but many failed when the time came to start making the loan repayments.

'Ideal' conditions for high gearing are a stable market with a predictable future, little competition, high margins, and a solid asset base, but then, these are ideal conditions for any business!

WHERE TO NEXT?

Selling at discounts on extended credit can be a disaster (Chapter 4)

Fluctuations in price are critical in the gearing equation (Chapter 5)

Genuinely loyal customers can reduce the risk from gearing (Chapter 9)

Controlling money is a *sine qua non* for business (Chapter 20)

16. Profit – revenue minus expenses

Profit is the measure with which the performance of a business is valued by investors and taxed by government. Otherwise, it may be ignored – or is it also a primary mechanism for managing people?

The great majority of people working in business are not overly concerned with profit, it is just something that happens, often in mind-boggling numbers. Any individual person's contribution, even if it were measurable, is swamped. People setting out in business for themselves tend to ask two questions – at the outset: 'How much profit should we expect to make?' and, after a period of trading: 'Where is it then?'

Neither question is easy to answer, but the second can at least be interpreted; it often means: 'The accountant has said we have made a profit, so why is there no money in the bank?' The explanation is that profit is not necessarily cash.

Accounting profits

There is something definite about cash.[1] Something called a bank statement provides immutable, independent evidence of its existence. Provided it is error-free, you can't argue with a bank statement. Profit however, as measured in the accounts of a business – the bottom line of the Profit and Loss account – is the result of a number of conventions. It is noteworthy that the definition of business in Chapter 1 does not include the word 'profit', and indeed, in a world without taxes, an independent business could continue quite happily without knowing whether it made an accounting profit, so long as it always had enough cash to pay bills and the proprietor's wages. The Inland

---

[1] In accounting terminology, 'cash' normally means money in the bank.

Revenue thinks differently, and insists on a profit calculation which it uses as a basis for corporation tax on companies and schedule D income tax on unincorporated businesses. Self-employed people generate profits from their trade or profession which are subject to taxation independently of how much they transfer from the business to their personal bank accounts.

Another group of people are interested in profits, namely those individuals and executives who are collectively known as the stock market. They like to see the companies in which they invest showing profits. Economists have long since recognised that cash is ultimately what matters for any size of firm, and the more applied amongst them have developed theories that the stock market value of a firm is equal to the discounted value of all its future cash flows. The stock market, meanwhile, continues to think that the price of a share should be some multiple of its earnings per share, which is, roughly speaking, the accounting profit divided by the number of shares in existence. This multiple is called the P/E or Price-Earnings ratio.

The interests of these various bodies give rise to potential accounting schizophrenia in that, from a perspective of liability to taxation the firm would naturally enough want to show the lowest possible profits. On the other hand, from a perspective of obtaining the highest share price, the profits should be as great as possible. Private firms, mostly but not exclusively small, tend to follow the former route, and ideally would like to prepare a different set of accounts for the Inland Revenue than for their bank manager. (To some extent, this has been achieved in effect by the preference of the bank to lend on the basis of cash flow forecasts.) It is said that before Manchester United Football Club received a stock market listing, the chairman's principle objective was to avoid paying corporation tax. In those days, the sale and purchase of players were shown as entries in the Profit and Loss account, so, to avoid tax, Man Utd would simply buy some more players! Now that it is a quoted company, it wants to show itself in the best light which, as for other listed firms, means reporting good profits. (Interestingly, its football results are better as well.)

The above hints that manipulations of profit figures take place, and they do – but this is a whole area beyond our current scope. Even before any creative accounting takes place, profit is a dangerous concept, because it is part of the going concern principle. Profit is the difference between *revenue and expenses.* Revenue is income generated from sales to customers, but they do not need to have paid for their purchases to be counted. Under principles of accrual accounting, sales take place at the point the customer takes delivery of the goods, and this is counted in the accounting period when it happens. Expenses, for the Inland Revenue's purposes, must be incurred 'wholly and exclusively' for the purpose of the associated sale, and while the accounting definition may perhaps be a little looser, it is entirely possible that the firm has incurred other expenses which are not part of this profit calculation. The obvious case is where the firm has obtained or produced a large quantity of *stock*, which, on the principle that it will one day be sold, is given a value that could not be instantly realised. Methods of valuing stock are to some extent flexible, and with enough flexibility, a range of profit figures can potentially be produced. With small firms, the Inland Revenue has the advantage of statistical information from many tax returns and tends to query claims outside the usual range.

It is not unusual for the type of small firm owners who rely totally on their accountants to prepare figures for them, upon being told that they have made a profit, to ask where it is. With larger firms, year on year differences are usually proportionately smaller, and the working capital changes[2] mentioned above are more limited in their effect on the divergence between profit and cash. There is another respect in which profit differs from cash, that of the *depreciation charge*. This is included in expenses, but it is not a payment from the bank account. It is an adjustment for a payment that happened some time ago. Consequently, when other things are equal, profit understates the cash generated from trade. It is the convention amongst corporate strategists to talk of a company's cash flow, this not being a reference to the statutory document called the cash flow statement, but a more useful measure of what the business is actually achieving from its trading activities. In most cases, most of this will be reinvested to appear as growth in assets.

Levels of profitability

The use of depreciation in the calculation of profit introduces the notion of expected or useful life of the associated assets, but

---

[2] See Chapter 14 for a discussion of working capital.

the accounting treatment is essentially arbitrary, as it does not reflect, for example, the alternative uses to which the asset – or the cash it uses – might be put. The method of calculation which takes this properly into account, and the accepted theoretical method for evaluating an investment in a working asset is that of *discounted cash flow*. Estimates of future cash flows from and to the project in question are calculated, compared with the important starting point of what happens if the investment is not made.[3] The net cash flow for each time period is adjusted to a value in the present by means of a discount factor, and the sum total gives a *net present value*. (Think of a discount rate as the reverse of an interest rate. As a sum of money gets bigger in the future thanks to the interest rate, so a future sum gets smaller in the present via the discount rate.) The choice of discount rate is obviously important, and if a normal rate of return for a given industry can be identified and applied, then a normal project will yield a net present value of zero. Anything doing better than that is a project which should be undertaken. That is roughly how the theory goes though in truth, not every project is evaluated using discounted cash flow techniques.

The extension of this theory from the asset or project to the whole firm is relatively simple. The combined cash flows from the firm's activities are the sum total of its value; hence, it should be worth the discounted value of its future cash flows. Financial theorists have put much effort into trying to measure the normal levels of profit for an industry, since these will provide objective measures which can be used to determine appropriate discount rates. Yet, like the new owner-manager's first question, this is easier asked than answered. The most interesting question when a project shows a positive net present value is: why? The result implies that the firm expects to do something that other firms do not, and identifying what this is becomes the major step along the way to ensuring that the firm can protect its ability to do it. Sometimes, the explanation will lie with some intellectual property such as a patent or proprietary technology; other circumstances may involve being ahead of competition and therefore able to charge higher prices for a while, or to secure the first and therefore best choice of

[3] This is not necessarily zero. For example, existing customers might be lost to a competitor unless a new facility is made available.

distribution channels. Often, though, it is more nebulous, just being 'better' – having a 'distinctive competence' – a concept at the heart of corporate strategy.

Owner-managed firms

There is no automatic right to make a profit in a small firm either, though often people assume that there is. It is common to see businesses for sale at a premium on the value of their assets (even when viewed as a going concern, and certainly at their market value), and this premium should represent the future earnings potential of the business. However, when asked why they are selling, the owners will often reply, 'Because I am not making any money.' The next question is obviously, 'Why then the premium?' to which the answer follows, 'Because I have worked very hard to get where I am.' The fact is, hard work is no guarantee of profit; it may possibly be a necessary condition in a small firm, but it is not sufficient.

The earnings of an owner-manager ought correctly to be viewed in two parts. As a manager, he or she should expect to earn what someone else would be paid to do the job; after that, if there is a profit, it should be a normal return on capital for an ordinary business, so it will not be all that great if only limited capital is involved. An unusual business might generate exceptional profits, and the same question should be asked of a business plan showing 'unusual' profits for a small firm (where cash flow forecasts are not usually discounted), namely: why? Commonly – too often perhaps – the reverse is the case. People go into business either without considering profit, or by allowing that a new business might make a loss in its early stages, they confuse this with not paying its manager. The business is not essentially viable because there are not enough customers and/or too much competition and/or not enough time to serve enough people, but the owner is denying the fact by not drawing the proper salary as the manager. Having to pay someone else to do the work would make it all too obvious. Hence, there is a last ditch and frequently doomed attempt to recover the real losses through the sale at a premium.

Acceptable returns

It is relatively easy to imagine how the level of profitability of a small firm might be determined by external factors such as the extent of local competition. Living in a community, one can observe firms entering and exiting the local market, being initially attracted by the profitability achieved by the other firms, only to add a little too much capacity themselves. For a while, everyone does badly until someone gives up or goes bust, and the pendulum swings again. For large firms, there is some statistical evidence about what constitutes a normal level of profit in a given industry, but investors seek better than this. They want the shares they have invested in to out-perform the market average. What is interesting about 'normal industry returns' is why they should be different for different industries (which they are), and why certain firms appear to be competent only at certain things.[4]

In the recession at the end of the 1980s, firms did 'get out' of lots of diversified business activity – mainly by selling the bits they did not want to other firms, the managers, or the public – while not necessarily staying in the most profitable, as measured by industry averages. The objective was to concentrate on – and stick to – what the firm identified as its core business, irrespective of its underlying level of profitability (as measured by the return on capital investment). There are exceptions, but mostly this is the business the firm has been in traditionally. Even the great Michael Porter was at a loss to explain why firms do not exit low return areas in favour of high ones. He put forward the idea of financial barriers to exit – firms did not leave because of what it would cost. The flaw was that because they did not leave, these costs were never identified, and therefore never proven to exist. Like the goblins at the bottom of the garden, a good reason for avoiding the bottom of the garden – and the goblins.

Profits and decisions

The Royal Commission which investigated UK small firms in the 1970s found that less than 10 per cent operated with a direct

---

[4] For example, the US Corporations Xerox and Land Polaroid both generated significant profits from their patented inventions but failed to develop effective real business streams.

objective of improving profits. Although this was a long time ago, there is no reason to suppose that things will have changed. It is true that banks appear more interested in cash flow (and correspondingly less in security against borrowings) than thirty years ago, when the norm was to lend against balance sheets, but there is no evidence that there is now a better survival rate of firms, for example. The underlying constant over the years is that small-firm owners regard themselves by their occupation first and as business managers second. The pursuit of 'business' really means the pursuit of more customers, more sales, with the assumption that profits will follow. This is the common expectation the Commission found, but, as demonstrated in Chapter 5, it is by no means a guaranteed conclusion. Too often, extra sales come from bigger discounts, longer credit terms, and extra work to deliver them resulting in increased overheads. The effect of lowering prices and increasing fixed costs is to push the breakeven point for the business further into the distance and, for the owner, to invite a nervous breakdown or other personal catastrophe.

The capital markets always want big firms to sustain their rates of growth, and the fact that this cannot be done indefinitely is disguised by the merger and acquisition process. With small firms, there may well be a distinct choice between growth and profit maximisation. There is certainly a choice between reinvesting any spare cash and taking it out of the business, and there are other choices about capacity. Having spare capacity, so that new customers can be accommodated comfortably without increasing overheads, must underlie any growth strategy. Capacity could be physical, temporal, or human, and probably all three. Spare management resource may be needed to undertake research, identify new sources of profitable customers (because obtaining new business at any cost is not the route to successful growth), prepare new facilities, design new products, etc. To do this, profits that would otherwise accrue are sacrificed and cash is used up. Maximising profits on the other hand involves using every bit of available capacity, as discussed in Chapter 6.

Profits and budgets

It requires a subtle mind to appreciate that 'investment' in the spare capacity that promotes growth is in fact a way of using the profits that would have been made otherwise. People seem to find adjusting to the profit concept difficult. Leaving aside the accounting complexities, the common budget which itemises future revenues and expenses is essentially a profit forecast. Clearly, this is a most valuable tool in helping to identify what actions are likely to produce which results, but the realities of using budgeting are something of a nightmare.

Firstly people seem to have a predilection either for creating revenue (never minding the expense) or for controlling expenditure (forgetting about sales). It is not clear where this comes from, whether it is innate, acquired during infancy, or developed during first exposure to the commercial world, but it is rare for people to operate in both modes simultaneously, which is what managing a profit centre – being responsible for both revenues and expenses – entails. Apart from anything else, it is, for example, difficult to assess in advance whether a few days spent obtaining quotations will result in a better, cheaper micro-computer, or whether getting the new machine quickly and using it to write a sales proposal is the more effective use of time. This is why 'default' behaviour, or 'do what we always do' is so common. The culture of the firm takes over, and people follow sets of norms which are not designed – and not the most desirable – from a profit-generating perspective. One of these is requiring staff to prepare elaborate documentation for expense claims, something they typically do in working time and which their bosses then have to spend a commensurate time examining, in the belief that this is somehow making the staff more accountable – and effective. Perhaps the commonest horror is that of spending all the approved expenditure each year in case the budget is cut for the following year. This is particularly bad if the budget manager spends nervously and inadequately during the course of the year and thus under-performs in effectiveness, only to dispose of the balance in an urgent flurry as the year end approaches.

While anyone is making decisions which have effects within a market system, they really should consider beforehand the impact of any action on the firm's profitability, and, after the event, review the consequences. Life may be too short to do this all the time, but if decisions and actions are to remain consistent, some form of feedback is necessary – and in the case of businesses, this means reviewing the financial effects. The word *control* appears in this context, but usually with strong connotations of restriction of freedom, authority and spending power. It does not need to be interpreted in this negative way – there can be positive aspects of the concept, such as in the control exerted by a racing driver. Where there is no control, though, there is unlikely to be much sense.

The pub opposite one of our training venues brewed its own beer. The landlord had the promotional idea of selling pints of it at half price until seven o'clock, presumably reckoning that early customers might occasionally drink themselves into a protracted session. However, he also reckoned that he was not making much money, so he employed no staff during the happy hour period. As a result, it took ages to get served, so that people consistently failed to drink that extra cheap pint which might have made the difference to them staying the rest of the night.

A knitwear company successfully cleared many years' worth of unsold end-of-ranges using local newspaper inserts inviting people to visit the temporary store in its warehouse. This proved successful because prices were at clearance levels. Management was sufficiently impressed with the sales volume that it started manufacturing specially for this outlet – which was of course a disaster. These are examples, in their own way, of 'woolly thinking' where a specific objective is misinterpreted because its original rationale has been forgotten.

Artificial 'profit and loss' systems

At the BBC, a system of budgeting for accountability was introduced in the early 1990s, a necessary component of an internal market system which was intended to make staff of the Corporation aware of how much things cost, and thus show that they spent the licence income responsibly and efficiently. This was not the only imposed 'market system' to experience difficulty, for market systems tend to require regulation if they are to work for the benefit of the many and not the few.

At the BBC, it was determined that physical accommodation should be costed, and where the Corporation owned freehold buildings, the equivalent market rent should be used. This is potentially a nonsense, because one reason for owning property is that it is cheaper than renting it. Otherwise, how do property companies make profits? Some budget centres worked out that it would be cheaper to move out of BBC premises, but this route had to be denied to them, since a move to rented accommodation would obviously result in overall increased expenditure. So much for freedom of choice.

In the case of the Television Centre, there was no market rent, since there is no other organisation in the UK which would want such a building. Instead of realising that this gave the BBC a major scale advantage over other TV businesses (namely that it was big enough to afford its own TV centre which cost only maintenance) the powers-that-were insisted on allocating the TV centre a cost that would apply if it were an office building. The result was that budget holders shrank the space they used, and producers started hiring external studios, leaving their own empty. It is pretty fundamental to the market system that the achievement of economies of scale through investment in production facilities results in a lower overall cost position, an advantage actually denied to the BBC by its own 'market system'.

It not known how the decision about the TV Centre was taken, whether by an individual or a committee, but whoever it was should realise that to play God requires not just omnipotence but also omniscience. A depressing aspect of this whole process is that the Corporation was advised throughout by the consultancy wings of two of the world's largest accountancy firms, who should have cut their teeth on accounting for profits. Such nonsense is still about. A recent news item reported that the new system of internal charges for the BBC's record library meant that any programme maker wanting to use the same CD twice would find it cheaper to buy from a shop, which was exactly what was happening – several times over!

Budgets and targets

There is a theoretical method of budgeting which allows for the objective evaluation of any outcome, using principles known as flexible budgeting and variance analysis. A flexible budget is used to calculate exactly what should have been expected for a given level of output, and the variance analysis then examines how each category varied, according to its usage (that is, whether more or less of something was used than expected), and also its price (and any unexpected changes). This distinguishes between factors within and without the manager's control, and it also identifies efficiencies as well as overspends, which are the normal focus of budgetary review. In particular, it is acceptable under flexible budgeting to overspend in a given category if output is above the base forecast, provided the increased usage is in line with the revised performance. This remains a largely theoretical method, however, since allowing people to set their own levels of performance (which is essentially what the approach does) is not generally deemed to be acceptable by managers, directors and investors alike.

In the selling environment, people have to have targets. Budgets are what they are expected to achieve, and targets – naturally higher – are what they are set to achieve. They know they are not going to achieve their targets, but they accept them anyway. If anyone does achieve a target, what does that say about the manager who was prepared to let the person under-perform? When profit centre managers first produce their budgets, they are usually told that their sales are too low, and their costs too high. They know this, so before they prepare their budgets, they understate their sales, and overstate their costs. As noted in Chapter 1, it is the presence of people that makes the real, working world of business complicated.

WHERE TO NEXT?

Selling without considering the effect on profit is foolish (Chapter 4)

Understand what is meant by a 'cost' before using it to compute a profit figure (Chapter 7)

Strategy is about identifying areas of superior profit potential (Chapter 11)

The information which accompanies the profit and loss account is the most valuable (Chapter 19)

Section 5

Intelligence at work

17. Forecasting – the search for wisdom

There is no substitute for working out, ahead of doing it, how much ***money*** *will come from* ***selling things****, and how much will be* ***spent in so doing***

An entrepreneur whose business had failed is supposed to have replied when asked why: 'Because I started believing my own cash flow forecasts.' If, to paraphrase the saying somewhat, it is true that wise men produce forecasts, but only fools believe them, what is the point in forecasting? Anyone who really could tell the future precisely would just enter the National Lottery. Well, venture capitalists are said to prefer to invest in individuals who have previously failed, because they are much wiser after the event. Individuals do not care to fail, however, and the point of preparing forecasts is to acquire *wisdom before the event.*

Experience is the usual source of wisdom. Someone receives new information which requires action to be taken, it is incorporated into existing knowledge, and whether or not the evaluation is a conscious process, a decision is made. Sometimes additional questions are asked first, about subjects determined by the decision-maker's experience. When the future is being contemplated – particularly where a new business venture is under consideration – no one may even know what questions should be asked. The process of forecasting leads to finding out which issues are more and which are less important, and to work out suitable questions and answers to them.

It is also necessary, where large employers are concerned, to have plans for the more mundane reason that you cannot wait until everyone comes to work before deciding what they should do. Forecasts are used to ensure that the plans are consistent with some expectation of future events outside the company. The ability to forecast probably contributes to the success of

Ford of Britain, but, in 1991, they lost over £900 million. There was nothing wrong with the original decision to follow their forecast of a buoyant market before the event, but one must ask how long they continued with it, given that the decline 'took them by surprise' as reports put it. The market gives signals about what is actually happening; if they are not as forecast, common sense tells you which figures you should believe. Henceforth presumably, experience will do likewise for the people who were involved at Ford.

Cash flow forecasting

Cash flow forecasting is arguably the most commonsense activity to be found in business. Not only is it common sense to do it in the first place, but the methods by which it is done are also pure common sense. Everyone knows that they have a responsibility to anticipate their future expenditure in order to make decisions about what they can afford currently, even if not everybody actually does this all the time. This kind of responsibility increases considerably when it is on behalf of a business, where the flow of money is akin to that of a bloodstream. The only real difference between forecasting personal and business cash flows is that in the former the income is usually fixed, and the expenditure may have to be curtailed accordingly. In a business, if there is no expenditure, there may well be no income.

The thing that is not immediately sensible about cash flow forecasting is the name. 'Cash' actually means *money in the bank* in this context – the complete opposite of what the word means in the expression 'to cash a cheque' in fact. This is one of a number of English words which have been given a special meaning by the accountancy profession – 'folding stuff' is usually called *petty cash*. The *cash flow statement* which appears with statutory accounts has a slightly different meaning again, and it is looking backwards, not forwards. Cash flow forecasting means 'predicting future movements in and out of the bank account'.

Unlike other, historical, financial statements, there are no legal requirements or guidelines as to what a cash flow forecast should look like. Large companies will have their own printed special formats and software templates for internal use. Often departmental managers will have to prepare only budgets, leaving their financial colleagues to worry about bank balances. Banks have printed forms for business customers, but are quite happy to work with customers' own versions.

The usual convention when funds are being sought is to prepare a grid on a large sheet of paper. Each row represents a different category of revenue or expenditure, and each column a different month. Values are entered to represent the receipts and payments to be expected, and the two sets of figures for income and outgoings are totalled. The latter is then subtracted from the former to leave the *net cash flow* for the month. Essentially, it is as simple as that.

The cumulative effect of each month's net cash flow shows what the bank balance will be, and if this goes negative, the need to borrow is indicated. Loans for the capital base of the business and their repayment installments are usually included in the in-and-out sections, but the timing of repayments may have to be adjusted, as will the interest charges, as a result of the calculations. Because you do not know what the monthly balance will be before you start, the consequence of doing the first forecast is that you usually have to revise your original plans. It follows that cash flow forecasting is a circular process; final versions often look very different from first drafts.

'Special' versions are sometimes prepared for bank managers, showing a picture they will be happy with, but there is a danger in this. The cash flow forecast is certainly used to raise finance; indeed, it should be the centre of a business plan, with the written part explaining and justifying the numbers in the forecast. However, the forecast should also be the author's best estimate of what is going to happen. It follows that the author should be the person who will make the subsequent decisions which are based on the forecast.

Human scale

Big companies do not normally encounter difficulties managing cash flow (although Saatchi & Saatchi did in 1990), and the full detail of say British Telecom's cash flow would probably boggle the mind of anyone. Nevertheless, someone charged with the responsibility of managing a business unit should be able to reduce the complexity of affairs to a level where a cash flow forecast is helpful, even if it is not required by head office finance division. The cash flow begins with a *sales forecast*, which makes certain important assumptions about customers (of which more later). The patterns of buying behaviour will imply a whole series of activities which have to be undertaken in consequence. There are materials or stock to be purchased, staffing and resource plans to be determined. Physical capacity needs are implied by the sales pattern and, in fact, a series of hour-by-hour task lists and job descriptions can be prepared, and so on. It may also be necessary to generate the sales in the first place, using marketing and sales campaigns. The forecast becomes a *model* of the various activities in the business, showing how they fit together, and what the financial consequences will be. It the latter are not acceptable, the whole process has to be revised.

For people planning their own businesses, doing this can be the most wonderful experience, for all their intentions for different aspects and components – usually developed in isolation from each other – are brought together into a holistic view of events. The plan for the business takes on a new, multi-dimensional reality, and a form of 'dialogue' develops between the author and the forecast. If you have ever prepared a serious cash flow forecast, you are likely to recognise this notion. If not, you may well be sceptical. It is, after all, just a series of numbers on a piece of paper; you could put anything down.

Well, this is true – in fact, putting numbers down which are not totally random, but are, for example, what you would like to happen (rather than what you may expect) is a perfectly acceptable way of starting the process, because of its iterative nature. Usually, people begin it as a means of raising money, only to find it becoming a mechanism for taking decisions. Many are the sceptics who have had to be coerced or cajoled into starting cash flow forecasts, only for the process to take them over.

Perhaps the best test of this 'creed' occurred when teaching the inaugural class of Master of Business Administration students in the newly-independent, former Soviet Republic of Kazakhstan. Following the popular rejection of the USSR, the whole concept of planning (as in central planning) was discredited, inflation was running at 50 per cent a month, and there was no culture of finding things out (keeping secrets, or better still, not knowing any, was the norm). Against such a background, what chance a business plan based on a cash flow forecast? Fortunately, my colleagues and I had the sanction of course marks to get the students' attention, and, after showing how it was done, we set them to produce their own forecasts, using their own data. I am pleased to say that the results were excellent, several people said it was the best thing they had learned in the whole course, and a few went on to set up businesses. If you are still in doubt, my advice is to try it for yourself.

Preparing cash flow forecasts

If you are proposing to prepare a forecast, here are some tips:

- You will only learn from the experience if you do it yourself.
- Although it is very tempting to use a spreadsheet program, it can be difficult to follow the relationships you are setting up. To best understand what is happening, prepare your early forecasts by hand, perhaps moving to the spreadsheet at the fine-tuning stage.
- Prepare or obtain blank grids in advance; use pencil (you will make mistakes) and have a rubber handy (you will also change your mind).
- Keep it simple, otherwise the arithmetic will be overwhelming.
- Use round numbers, and if you have lots of small expenses to include, work them out on a separate sheet and use subtotal figures in your main plan; the big numbers are the most important.
- Check the arithmetic by adding across then down as well as down then across; you should get the same figure.
- Don't spend too long at one session; keep fresh.
- Keep two sets of notes as you proceed: one of the assumptions you make, the other of the things you need to investigate; priorities will emerge naturally.

Budgeting

The differences between financial forecasting using cash flows and forecasting based on budgets are mainly technical. *Budgets* record when a cost is to be incurred, rather than when it will be paid for. An annual insurance premium for example would show as a single payment in one month in a cash flow; in a budget, one-twelfth of the amount would appear each month, spreading the cost over a year.

It is important to recognise when a cost is *incurred*, as distinct from when it is *paid for*. Turning on a light incurs a cost as electricity is consumed, though it may be some time before the bill arrives, and a while later before it is settled. Uncontrolled consumption can lead to cash flow problems later (as when heavy winter heating bills arrive during Easter holidays), so once a cash flow forecast has been finalised, it is a sensible extension to convert it to a budget, and use both documents to take decisions. Commitments to future liabilities need to be recognised as they occur, but the ability to settle them when they fall due should also be considered. Except when it is expressed differently in the terms of trade, where goods are involved, the moment the cost is incurred is deemed to be the point the buyer takes delivery.

Some banks produce forms with spaces to record what actually happens against cash flow forecasts, but this activity is not much use. There could be two distinctly different reasons for outgoings being lower than forecast – because you did not incur an expected cost, or because you did, but can't afford to pay the bill! Broadly speaking, cash flow is a better tool for planning, and a budget is a better form of control. Recording the actual cost against the budget is immensely valuable, both for controlling expenditure and improving forecasting accuracy. Choosing the time to pay a particular bill can sometimes be a matter of discretion.

Organisational budgeting – where managers obtain approval for annual expenditure limits – is a different kettle of fish. It may start off as a form of forecasting, but it usually turns into a bidding, lobbying and manoeuvring exercise, with political skills dominating. It requires a philosophical debate to establish whether there are better ways of deciding how funds should be allocated and spending controlled amongst a large collection of people. It could be argued that the most able managers are those who succeed in obtaining the greatest spending power. However, their competences in so doing do not seem to be based in the actual *business* of the organisation. Too often, the annual budgeting round seems to interrupt, even suspend buying and selling activity, only to result in an ill-considered flurry as the year end approaches. You do not catch entrepreneurs spending money for the sake of 'preserving' the budget.

Discounted cash flow

This expression does not mean that cash flow should be ignored, of course; rather, it refers to the sophisticated economic process of evaluating alternative capital investment projects, whereby cash flows associated with each project are forecast, in the manner just described, but probably quarterly rather than monthly, and the total net cash flow for each period calculated. The intention is not to raise finance, this is assumed to be available; rather, it is to decide which investment(s) to pursue. A rate of return sought by the company (the discount rate) is used to equate a future cash flow to a value in the present, and the overall effect gives a *Net Present Value* for each of the projects, with the highest receiving the funding. As an alternative, an *Internal Rate of Return* may be calculated which, as it were, smoothes out the cash flows to give rates which can be compared instead of values.

Financial theorists have developed detailed mechanisms for determining appropriate discount rates, the theory being that there are two elements that make up the risk associated with the project. One part is the risk that is inherent in being involved in the industry, the environment and the world surrounding the project, and this is called the *systematic* risk, to reflect which a suitable discount rate can be computed using independent data. The other element is the *specific* risk for the particular project, and this is deemed by the theory to have been fully investigated by the management team preparing the cash flow forecasts. In a theoretical, perfect world, all available information has been incorporated into the forecasts, all of which have been prepared under comparable sets of assumptions.

This has a validity if alternative projects are actually being compared, but it is often the case that individual investments are subjected to this process. As they say in the computer industry, garbage in, garbage out, so, if the forecast cash flows are garbage, sophisticated computation of a discount rate will make no material difference, and attention is being paid to the wrong end of the equation. The chances are that any major investment big enough to warrant discounted cash flow evaluation is going to have a significant impact on its marketplace, likely to change its nature. The effect of this cannot easily be forecast, because it will probably induce competitive reactions, the nature of which the competitors themselves cannot predict until the event occurs, unless they have a predetermined set of responses for every contingency. Using management consultants to ask competitors what they would do is not really helpful, because you cannot assemble the group of people who would actually take the decision – and, if you could, do you think they would tell you?

Comparing alternative investments under different sets of assumptions can be done, and if a particular one is consistently ahead, that should be the choice. Usually, two scenarios (an optimistic and a pessimistic) would be the limit, if only because of the work involved. The point really is that major projects are actually undertaken by big businesses as part of a strategic commitment, rather than on a purely economic evaluation. The forecasts are reviewed and revised until acceptable financial consequences are projected. (The parallel for the small trader is to revise the projections until the level of overdraft is acceptable to the bank manager.) The difference in the big business is that it takes more people to manipulate the cash flow forecasts. The wisdom they acquire in the process is not usually available for the people who end up running the subsequent project, who may find the reality something of a shock. On the other hand, as Eurotunnel has demonstrated, banks are unlikely to foreclose on multibillion pound projects.

Sales forecasting

A detailed cash flow forecast should be fairly robust in the sense that if it is well planned, the numbers should add up more than just arithmetically, as it were. The activities they represent should make achievable – and preferably demonstrable – sense, always provided the sales pattern happens as forecast. The cash flow is saying, 'If it happens like this, this is how the business will function.' The sales forecast cannot be guaranteed, though – indeed, the word 'forecast' is specifically avoided in share prospectuses.

There are considerable differences in sales forecasting for the steady state compared with a new venture. You would expect next year's sales for a chain of newsagents to be pretty similar to this year's, for example; there might be the occasional changes at one or two stores caused by a competitor closing down or starting up, or a new one-way system affecting trade, but on average, such differences will be small. In contrast, a new independent newsagency will be difficult to prepare a reliable forecast for. It cannot be tested out in advance, and there is no point in asking people if they will use it (they do not know themselves, so what they say will not be meaningful). Opening it is really an act of faith. It is unlikely that there is a totally untapped demand for newspapers etc, so the forecast will be based on assumptions about *changes* in potential customers' shopping habits, which are notoriously difficult to anticipate. (For the record, news wholesalers are reluctant to supply new retailers, as one too many in a given area can make them all unprofitable.)

Steady state forecasting, where next year will be much like this, is a prime subject of 'management science'. Sophisticated mathematical techniques can be used to examine trends over time, for example, and thereby attempt to improve the accuracy of forecasts. Getting the final few percentage points right can be a great source of efficiency in large scale operations, and well worth the effort, therefore. Such models are usually built purely on sales data, and do not refer to the first principles of customer buying patterns. Economic forecasting models are usually a series of regression equations which have no physical meaning. Probabilities are also used, where the expected value of a contract is its total multiplied by a percentage reflecting the chances it will be awarded. This can be useful for financial planning, but, in the actual event, the business either gets the contract one hundred per cent, or it does not.

The importance of customers

Statistical approaches do not create problems if buying patterns are well insulated from external factors which could cause them to undergo fundamental change. Still, forgetting about the existence of customers can lead to unwise decisions. Government statisticians always quote unemployment figures 'seasonally adjusted' as this is a sensible way of comparing them month by month. Some time ago, they were also quoting figures seasonally adjusted for the numbers of tourists visiting the UK, which is a singularly unhelpful thing to do. From a business perspective, the pattern of seasonality associated with tourism is one of the most vital considerations. Smoothing out the variations would lead to undercapacity in the peaks and thumb-twiddling in the troughs.

One of the more famous failures to remember the customer happened when wide-bodied jets were introduced into service in the US. Where two airlines were flying between the same pair of cities (a common occurrence), there was a well-known relationship called the S-curve, whereby the carrier with the larger share of the capacity on the route had a more than proportionate share of the passengers. Now, capacity is measured in available-seat-miles, and some airlines worked out that if they used wide-bodied jets, they could increase their share of the passengers while at the same time reducing some of their costs by operating fewer flights. Four wide-bodied flights of 250 seats could replace six of 120, for example. There was genuine surprise when the carriers that did this found they were actually *losing* share to those who did not.

As a passenger, you can probably work out what had happened. Passengers are not especially interested in the number of seats on the plane, but they do care about its departure time. The operationally-oriented industry (which is now much more customer aware) saw one variable as *capacity*, but it was actually *number of flights* (there being a perfect correlation between the two when the planes are the same size) which affected the passengers. Reducing the number of flights had lost market share; given the price of jumbo jets, this was an expensive oversight.

Forecasting change

The sales forecast for a new venture has to be based on an anticipation of how customers will behave, and it needs to be closely monitored once the venture starts trading. It is not just *whether* a satisfactory level of sales can be achieved that matters, the vital question is *how long it will take* for the level to be reached. Some businesses, usually those that do not require physical resources, can be arranged to trade profitably from day one, but most do not. The loss-making period at the beginning can have a significant impact on the overall amount of capital required, and not even a proportion of it is recoverable if the venture has to be abandoned. (Plant and equipment can at least be sold second hand.)

The expectations of what constitutes a reasonable forecast are dependent upon the business in question. The *degree* and *frequency* of *repeat purchasing* by customers are key factors. To demonstrate this, consider the planning process for a small hairdressing salon.

Suppose the hairdresser will make an adequate profit from 30 appointments a week. How many clients are then required? The answer is not 1,560 a year (being 30 times 52 weeks); most people are loyal to one hairdresser, and pay considerably more than one visit a year. If the average person attends every 4 weeks, then only 4 × 30 = 120 clients will be needed to support the business. The problem is getting them. The assumption of their loyalty to the new salon implies that they have to be wooed away from their current hairdresser, which will not be easy. The new salon needs a marketing strategy to encourage people to try it. Introductory offers will attract people to the salon, but the more enticing they are made, the less interested the people enticed will be in the service itself, and the lower the 'conversion rate' to regular clients will become.

The sales forecast may then be based around the assumptions that for example 20 new people per week can be attracted, of whom 2 will become regular clients, and one of each two can be relied on to introduce a friend. To prepare the forecast properly, it is necessary to write everything out on a suitable schedule; there will obviously be a time at which the salon starts to be too busy to have 20 newcomers a week, and care will be needed to ensure that regulars are not the people taking up the promotions, etc, etc. For our purposes here, we can work out that 120 clients can be made up from 80 recruits plus 40 friends they introduce. At a rate of 2 a week, it will take 40 weeks to achieve the target. This will also mean attracting 40 × 20 = 800 people into the salon; if this is expected to cost £10 per head say, then the marketing budget to establish the business will need to be £8,000.

Once trading begins, the proprietor will need to monitor the accuracy of the assumptions. Merely counting results will not mean much unless they are referred back to the original 'equations' – it is the *relationship between the variables* rather than the values they assume which matters. If you understand the *algebra* of the system, you can adjust your plans and actions accordingly. In the salon, if only one person out of 20 converts, the proprietor has to decide whether to wait 80 weeks to achieve target, or to change the direction of the promotion; if everyone is introducing a friend, the marketing budget can be reduced (or some of it spent to reward them). If the average repeat is 3 weeks, then 90 clients will be enough, and so on.

Other businesses behave quite differently from hairdressers, and there is no alternative in sales forecasting but to start with the *expected pattern of customer behaviour* for the particular business. Because of the difficulty of recruiting a loyal client base, hairdressers usually start by working for someone else. Osteopathic practitioners do not, and as the majority of their clients have an occasional rather than a chronic need for treatment, it can take several years to establish a practice. Restaurants do not usually build up trade slowly, because an empty restaurant attracts no passing trade, and provides no ambience. They need to be launched, with a splash, and sometimes a number of false starts occur, though a short newspaper review can be enough to establish a restaurant for years. As a complete contrast, a gift shop in Stratford-upon-Avon should start trading at full level immediately it opens without publicity, if it sells solely to tourists. A moment's thought shows that, as they are strangers themselves, they will not know it is new.

WHERE TO NEXT?

Marketing campaigns kick off forecasts (Chapter 3)
The impact of pricing policies can be estimated (Chapter 5)
New ventures start with forecasts (Chapter 12)
Working capital requirements need forecasting (Chapter 16)

18. Researching realities

The prospects of ***selling things for more money*** *are enhanced when there is some certainty about how customers and competitors will react*

A lecturer from an economic forecasting unit once told a class of MBA students how the unit's latest forecast for growth in GDP had been out by two per cent. This produced a fair number of gasps from the class; two per cent is an impressively narrow margin of error. One more sceptical student asked what had happened exactly, whereupon the lecturer explained that the two per cent difference was between their forecast of three per cent, and the actual result of one per cent. Note the distinction; the margin was two percentage points perhaps, but in effect the forecast was wrong by 200 per cent.

Such inaccuracies have not prevented economic forecasters from establishing relationships with a wide range of customers, including governments. There are many decisions to be taken about the future, which would be random choices without indications of what lies ahead. Imagine the Chancellor of the Exchequer delivering a budget speech proposing a tax on say, the importation of private cars, or the sale of home-made jam, accompanied by the words, 'We don't know how much this will raise, but we think it is a jolly good idea.' He must believe the figures provided by the Treasury – or at least give the appearance of so doing – when he sets out to manage the Nation's finances.

Perhaps the task is hopeless, though. In 1987 Peter Drucker claimed that economics had failed. Marxist economics definitely failed a few years later when the Soviet Union finally gave up the ghost. Market economics does not work either, he claimed; if it did, governments would be able to manage their economies. If you accept this view, and also that economics is an internally consistent, rigorous discipline, then its failure must lie in the assumptions upon which the theories are developed. This is easy to see in some instances such as cost benefit analysis, where complex arithmetical calculations are performed on nearly arbitrary data gathered by asking people how much they would pay to save a Norman church from demolition, or a rare species of toad from extinction. The assumption that all judgments are translatable into a monetary equivalent – the view that everyone and everything has a price – is not justified.

This creates a general problem for researchers, for their best results are obtained if they start with theories and assumptions, which then direct their attention towards what precisely to observe. The instructions, 'Go out and research butchers,' ought to elicit the response, 'Why?' Adding the purpose: 'to find out if they are suffering from competition by supermarkets' makes the task realisable. In pure science, there have been major discoveries from unexpected events, such as Rutherford 'splitting the atom' where the result was likened to 'a cannonball bouncing off a sheet of tissue paper'. In the social sciences, where there is so much to observe in so little time, a subject or observation which does not 'fit' tends to be ignored in favour of those that do. Unstructured detailed research gathered by telephone always shows a bias towards the people with strong opinions, as they are more likely to answer questions about a topic if it interests them. When there is no opinion, there is nothing much to say, and this applies for most people to most things they have not previously thought about, including the plight of rare species. How exactly could you really measure the price of saving the toad from extinction – hold a Toads-in-Need pledge auction on TV?

Even when people think they know their opinions, they can be wrong. The opinion polls for the 1997 general election got it wrong again. Their famous failure to name the correct government in 1992 seemed not to deter them; it was accepted in some quarters that people changed their minds at the very last minute. In 1997 the polls were in a sense just as inaccurate. The five leading surveys for the broadsheet newspapers just about averaged between them the correct figure for the Conservative share of the total vote, but their average overstated the Labour share by 12 per cent,[1] with the nearest figure being 6 per cent too optimistic.

Pollsters make matters worse for themselves by adjusting

---

[1] The percentage is the proportionate difference, not the error. The polls forecast a share between 46 per cent and 50 per cent; it turned out to be 43 per cent.

results to exclude the undecided, as if somehow to claim that their polling methods are reliable – or they would be were it not for the silly people who cannot make up their minds. Perhaps their customers – the media – do not fancy publishing uncertain headlines such as 'Tories might not be leading'. The fact of democracy is that the undecided are just as entitled to vote as the committed, and are more likely to swing the result on a first past the post system. If anything, they are more, not less, important. In business, you would be particularly interested in people with unformed opinions because these represent the best opportunities for growth.

Growth rates and limits

It is when growth is projected that the difference between 6% and 12% really shows. If these percentages are annual growth rates, the divergence is massive. Something growing at 6% compound doubles in size after about 12 years, by which time 12% growth would have reached almost 4 times its original size. After only 5 years, 6% produces growth of one third; 12% increases the original by three quarters. In terms of sales forecasting and capacity planning, these differences are significant indeed.

Compound growth is used in forecasting because where growth occurs in nature, it is usually exponential – meaning that the amount of a growth is proportionate to the size of the thing at the time. Plants grow this way, their ability to do so being a function of the number of cells available to divide. There are many circumstances in which markets grow similarly, particularly when new consumers are being added each year, and consumption is spreading. However, plant growth does not continue for ever, and nor does market growth. There are two questions in any calculation of growth patterns – what will the rate be, and how long will it last? If you should come across expensive published market research reports which have impressive-looking tables of market size up to the year 2020, look carefully at the text. If it states: 'the market is expected to grow at x%', you may find you can calculate the numbers in the tables for yourself. Beware, because we can be almost certain that the one thing the market will *not* do is to grow at the same rate for the next twenty years.

The assumption of limitless growth seems to be far too common, perhaps because 'preparing for the end' is against human nature. The problem comes home to roost with one-product, or specialised companies. In the early days of the now defunct Unlisted Securities Market, it admitted a company with an impressive growth rate making toasted sandwich machines. These devices had recently captured the public imagination, and this firm were market leaders. Of course, once people owned one toasted sandwich machine, they did not require another, so the pattern of growth ceased abruptly. During the late 1980s, fitted kitchens became the fashion, creating lots of opportunity for design and installation companies. Once a family had a new fitted kitchen, it was unlikely to want another for a while, so the design companies went bust. In the mid-1990s, mountain bike companies suffered – because lots of people owned mountain bikes.

Diffusion of innovations

Products which follow this general pattern of speedy acceptance as people, households or firms acquire one and then do not need another for a while – or possibly ever – follow a fairly standard pattern known as a diffusion curve. Graphically, this looks like a normal distribution curve, shaped like a section through a bell, showing volume sales plotted against each time period. The initial slow take-off (through enthusiasts and experimenters) gathers momentum as the population at large start to encourage each other in various ways. A large number of factors are involved, ranging from wider distribution and cheaper prices, to pressure from the children to keep up with their friends. Sales peak at the point when about half the final penetration has been reached, and decline symmetrically with their growth. If the time period and final penetration figure can be estimated, a curve can be constructed, and a reasonable forecast produced.

Thus, consideration of the market for karaoke holograms would start with an assessment of the rate of diffusion of KHPs,[2] accompanied by a further assumption about the number of holo-

---

[2] A KHP is a *karaoke hologram player*, a device which enables people to 'perform' as their particular hero alongside a projection of the rest of the band. It does not exist.

grams to be sold per year per installed KHP. As the markets for home technology-based products are global, key research topics on the supply side can be identified and undertaken. First, what is the capacity for producing KHPs, and second, what new capacity is planned? It is pretty much a waste of time asking people if they will buy one,[3] but you can be fairly sure that if a business owns a factory producing them, it will try hard to sell them. What consumers talk *of doing* is meaningless, but what industrial competitors *are doing* is fact (even if the decisions to proceed are based on consumer research). The useful consumer research about the future[4] is not quantitative, but qualitative investigations which give clues as to how best to persuade people to become consumers.

The operative word is 'how'. Qualitative issues – how people feel about things, how they react to messages etc, and similar subjects – can be tested in advance and refined in practice. Access to the individual is important in qualitative research, and it needs to be conducted very carefully. Just asking people what they think will firstly confuse them, as their thoughts on this particular topic are not uppermost. Once this question is addressed – by getting people to partake in group discussions usually – they then tend to say *what they think* the hosts want to hear – but what their hosts want to hear is what their guests *feel*, not what they think. Such *focus groups* are usually organised with facilitators who are professionally qualified psychologists – and the agenda needs careful setting. Given the nebulous quality of feelings, obtaining usable results can be expensive. Alternatives are such things as competitions where entrants are invited to rank-order product attributes. These result in larger data sources, but whether the opinions are of ultimate value is not certain.

Gathering information

Whatever data is gathered, it is neutral; it is the use to which it is put that turns it into business research. Is the observation,

---

[3] They will say something like 'Probably, but it would depend on the price.'
[4] There is a massive amount of research into what consumers *have done*. See Chapter 9.

'There are no golf courses in Kazakhstan,' bad news for a golf club manufacturer looking for new markets? If no one plays, they will not want clubs – unless of course they take the game up, in which case it will be an excellent market. I once heard an airline pilot talking about colleagues who had set up businesses 'on the side'. Pilots typically are well paid, expect shorter than average careers, and work irregular hours, which makes it attractive for them to start their own businesses when an opportunity arises. In this instance, each opportunity mentioned was preceded in the pilot's words with 'a quick market study'. It became obvious that this particular aviator had no idea what a market study entailed, never mind a quick one. He seemed to think of it as a parallel with the safety procedures performed before a flight. Pilots work in a very precise world, and presumably expect to encounter similar precision in other walks of life. I imagine it was a major disappointment to him when he finally saw his first 'quick market study'. In flying terms, such a document might tell you your destination, but not your route.

Even the fastest growing markets can be bad environments in which to compete if the supply side is developing faster than the demand side, a phenomenon which is arguably on the increase with globalisation and extensive information exchange. If one firm can identify a potential growth area, so can its competitors. On the other hand, if the firm can identify where its competitors *are not going*, it has a better chance of finding some suitable space for itself. This means that research into competitor activity is not only based on fact, but it is also open to positive interpretation, and it is invaluable. Michael Porter's rise to pre-eminence amongst strategists arose from his course at Harvard Business School entitled 'Analysis of Industry and Competition'. This was a much desired course unit for people intending to join strategic management consultancy firms, much of whose work, under the banner of industry studies, involves interviewing their clients' competitors.

This is not to suggest that management consultants are the only source of competitor information. Industries vary in the extent to which they share information about future plans. A 1997 edition of *Autocar* magazine features the new Rover Mini, for example, even though it will not be on the market until 2000, since it is widely held that 'everyone would find out anyway' if it were kept secret. It is not obviously a straightforward task for a manager to ring up his counterpart in a rival firm and ask for corporate secrets to be disclosed, but a fair exchange of information is – well, a fair exchange, certainly if it involves swapping stories about third and fourth parties.

Expertise

So information circulates and, with much of it also published and otherwise disseminated, it is not difficult to gather knowledge. This is typically how the consultant would approach a competitor armed with data ready to trade, and to discuss interpretations of what is going on in the world of their shared interest. This is the reason given by the consultancy firms for employing high-powered, and highly-paid, MBAs to carry out the basic work of data collection, much of which is mundane; the analytical skills may be required at any moment to interpret a particular nugget of information which might otherwise be submerged in the routine.[5]

Many MBA courses include an element of project work, where students can cut their teeth on data collection. Some students assume that if they succeed in collecting a decent quantity of data, the rest will be plain sailing. The truth is different, for if there are to be conclusions drawn in a student project (that is, it is not just an exercise in data gathering) then a better scenario is that it only begins in earnest after the first information is to hand. Until that point, most projects are speculative; only as data emerges does the reality emerge – and with it, the real questions that need answers. Some people experience the same phenomenon with their PhDs, with the famous last words, 'Now I only have to write it up,' presaging the real heartache.

The other major lesson to be learned from project work is that if someone has already gathered the available data, there is no need to replicate their work, provided of course that they will allow you access to it. The chances are that if there is data readily available, someone will indeed have gathered it, and their living or reputation might well depend on their having done the work reliably. Of course, in some instances it might be

[5] Another reason might just be that recent graduates from places like Harvard Business School are capable of working at twice the rate of normal people.

necessary to pay for it, but there are other circumstances, such as the work of trade associations, where firms have subscribed in advance with just such a purpose in mind. If there is doubt about the reliability of any particular source, consultations with three or four good sources in the given field should show up any discrepancies. Basically, topics on which they concur can be taken as read, and though there is no underlying law which states it, this usually accounts for around 80 per cent of the total. All being well, this identifies the remaining 20 per cent as the interesting area for exploration. If you ask to use someone else's report,[6] remember that you do not have to accept the interpretations that go with it, only the data itself. The first question with any research project should therefore be, 'Does anyone else know?'

Speed

Time is usually important, since getting into a market first may offer opportunities for superior profits before competitors respond. (Sometimes, it does the opposite, with the first entrant bearing the brunt of the cost of educating the consumer etc, only for the competitors to reap the major harvest with superior, snag-free versions of the innovation. On balance, problems of this nature may encourage firms to cooperate over innovations as they all stand a better chance that way.) The speed of any research can make a difference, and just how not to go about it is demonstrated by a pointless practice to be found amongst venture capital companies. A glance through the directory of the British Venture Capital Association will reveal that besides the big investors like 3i, there are quite a number of small funds which claim to invest in only a tiny fraction of the proposals they scrutinise. This is probably because their practice, on receiving a business plan from a team of entrepreneurs, is to undertake their own independent industry research.

This is a stupid thing to do. If the investors know more about the industry than the entrepreneurs, they already know whether the business plan is any good. More to the point, they probably know that they do not want to invest because the entrepreneurs

[6] I am not suggesting that you should cheat as a student by using a colleague's work. The advice is to consult experts in their fields.

are not sufficiently well-informed to run the business. They should be experts, and if they know less than a venture capitalist, either they, or the venture person, is in the wrong job. So, the entrepreneurs start with more knowledge than the investors, which raises three questions: are they serious about their business plan, are they putting in their own money, and does the plan – the interpretation of the research data – make sense? References will help with the first question (it is necessary to avoid swindles), and the second (to be evidenced in due course) will show if they are serious. If they are competent, this will be apparent from their interpretation of the data, in which case it can be pretty safe to assume that they have conducted their research diligently. If the proposal is attractive in principle, now is not the time to beat about the bush. The chances are it will have gone to other potential investors, and they will not all make the same mistake.

WHERE TO NEXT?

Advertising benefits from research (Chapter 2)
Competitors' operational strategies affect delivery terms (Chapter 6)
And expectations generally (Chapter 11)
About expected levels of profitability (Chapter 16)

19. Information

Without information a business will have difficulty understanding what it ***sells*** *and what it* ***spends in so doing***

Information is valuable. There is a story that the fortunes of the Rothschild family were greatly improved by the careful use of information at the time of the Battle of Waterloo. Receiving advanced news by carrier pigeon of the likely outcome, a member of the family dutifully informed the King, but His Majesty was obliged to await confirmation of the news from official sources. Mr Rothschild meanwhile was able to instruct 'unreliable confidantes' to dispose of large holdings of government stock without letting the source be known. The unreliability of the confidantes was important, for others in the market quickly saw through the façade. The Rothschilds had something of a reputation for European influence (during the Peninsular War, they had managed to get money to the Duke of Wellington's troops who were on the verge of mutiny), and 'The City' now interpreted events to mean that the engagement at Waterloo had turned against Wellington. Consequently, they joined in the selling, and prices dropped abruptly – to the point where Rothschild (this time using reliable confidantes) was able to buy up masses of stock at rock bottom prices. When the official news from Waterloo finally landed, these same stocks hit an 'all time high'.

Carrier pigeons were the original means of information transfer used by Reuters, a company which now numbers amongst the top 100 (a FTSE company) in the UK. Much of Reuters' income comes from supplying information to the financial markets. There are theories that financial markets are driven by information, including one that the price of a share reflects all that is currently known about that company. Those who believe that this knowledge is everything there is to know refer to something called the perfect market hypothesis. Those who deny this theory refer to the law (not of science, but of

Parliament) which makes insider trading (dealing in shares while party to privileged information not yet available to the market at large) a criminal offence. Financial markets may be based upon information, but they also involve a fair smattering of hearsay and supposition. A firm that under-performs in its sector should have a low share price – except that the price may rise in anticipation of it becoming a takeover target ('bid rumours', as they are known). Consequently, it does not become a takeover target because its shares are overpriced – and so on. What is true is that the price of a share normally reflects the point of neutrality – throughout the market, there is as much desire to sell as to buy the shares.

Confidentiality

The problem with information is that there is no known method of getting people to pay you for it after you have given it to them, unless you have an on-going relationship (such as a contract like Reuters', or perhaps the mechanisms police use with their informers). Consequently, important information may only be valuable when it is secret, for if disclosure gives away the secret, it may also give away the value. There is one of those stories (they always happen to a friend of a friend, never someone one actually knows) which tells that the person who suggested to the manufacturers of Swan Vesta matches how they could save money by putting sandpaper along one box edge only instead of two, received a substantial reward. If this is true, it depended entirely on the decency of the company – with no scruples, they might have been tempted to remark that they already had plans to do just that, thank you. For information to be of immediate value in business, there has to be some mechanism for converting it into money – some superior trading proposition, and it is normally the person who owns that mechanism who stands to benefit.

Unless information (in the nature of an idea) can be patented or otherwise protected from use by rivals, as soon as it is presented to the market in which it operates, it becomes more or less public knowledge, and competitors can imitate it. (This would be true for example if another match manufacturer attempted to compete with Swan Vesta by having lower costs through using only one strip of sandpaper. Once their product was launched, Swan Vesta would spot the difference.) When competitors respond, the usual outcome of market forces is that prices decline, or better performance is offered for the same price, and the ultimate beneficiary is the consumer. Generally, for this not to happen, competitors will have to collude, and this too is against the law.

Hence, the period of time between the launch of something new and its imitation is one that businesses look towards for extra profitability, and information about plans (sometimes taking on the form of industrial espionage), will be worth something for a critical period beforehand. Information about the strategies that different firms in similar industries are pursuing is similarly valuable, and their ability to gather this is possibly one of the reasons why strategic management consultancy firms can charge high fees.

Confidentiality thus becomes an issue, and while it would be nice to believe that all employees are loyal to their employers to the extent of keeping all confidences, the consensus tends to be that it is safer not to tell people unless they really have to know. This treatment of information is very much at odds with what is desired within organisations, for which the flow of information may be likened to a central nervous system which carries instructions to the workers and results of their achievements back to their managers. One rather silly case of confidentiality occurred at Saatchi & Saatchi during their period of massive expansion. Mainly, this growth came about through the acquisition of private firms (which are easier to buy for a target price if the deal is 'pre-emptive' – that is, if they don't see you coming). No one is quite sure how two Saatchi & Saatchi acquisitions teams happened to be operating independently in Ireland at the same time, but between them, they bought two advertising agencies in Dublin more or less simultaneously. These proceeded to compete with each other for business until someone found a method of politely disposing of one of them. This was not easy, because no one knew which was the 'wrong' one.

The problem of communication

The name may be vulgar, but no other term quite expresses the behavioural stresses generated by the ubiquitous phenomenon of the *Bloody Stupid Question* (BSQ). Common in owner-managed businesses, it appears as a part of a natural development process where, for all its apparent frustrations, it has an important role to play. The scenario is something like this:

At The Owner-Managed Business Ltd (TOMB)[1] it is the custom to obtain 10mm fossets from Castor Components Ltd. If the supplier is also out of stock, rather than hold up the production line, TOMB will buy from Pollux Fosset Supplies. Occasionally, the following conversation will ensue:

Tom (*the Owner-Manager*): What is it Jerry, I'm in the middle of something?

Jerry (*energetic, mouse-like senior employee*): Sorry to bother you boss, but Castor's are out of 10mm fossets. Shall I get some from Pollux?

Tom (*sarcastic*): No, there's a delivery due any minute by flying pig! (*Pause*) Of course you get 'em from Pollux. What a bloody stupid question!

* *

(*A few weeks later, Castor's are once again out of stock so Jerry takes the initiative. Tom walks through the assembly plant and calls Jerry into his office.*)

Tom: Sorry to interrupt you when you're hard at it, but aren't those Pollux fossets you're using out there? You know we use Castor's?

Jerry (*tempted to say something sarcastic, but thinking better of it*): Castor's were out of stock.

---

[1] This unfortunate acronym is lived up to by a subsection of owner-managers who really do seem to be trapped forever by their businesses. Learning to communicate – and so develop managers – is one possible escape route.

Tom: Fair enough.

Jerry: Is that all?

(*Walking back to his position, Jerry reflects that things are certainly not fair enough.*)

Jerry: What a bloody stupid question!

* *

Perhaps you recognise this scenario. If you feel that you recognise one side of it only, next time it happens, try and suspend the thoughts in your own head and think for a moment of the position others might be in. Not every Tom would wait to call Jerry into his office, instead blurting out the question there and then, adding amusement (or embarrassment, as the case may be) for the assembly workers looking on. What do people make of *you*?

What appears to be the commercial equivalent of a parent-adolescent spat is in fact an exchange of information. Jerry is not stupid, and he knows when to get Pollux fossets. He would not dream of holding up production because they are out of stock. He also knows that Tom *needs to be told*. The problem is that Tom is always wrapped up in what he is doing, and if Jerry just tells him casually, Tom will not remember. He therefore chooses to interrupt, thereby first gaining Tom's attention. This well-intentioned behaviour nevertheless earns some disapproval (the sarcastic comment), so when the situation occurs again, he acts. He might have told Tom what he'd done, but just telling him, the boss would not remember. Jerry would then have had to tell the boss he had told him, and so on.

Jerry is right of course – but so is Tom. When Tom sees them using Pollux fossets, he probably realises that Castor's must have been out of stock, but he still needs to know, so he speaks to Jerry about it. The effect of this is that the next time it happens, the chances are Jerry will interrupt Tom to ask about fossets . . .

Routines and review mechanisms

The worthwhile aspect of this seemingly pointless behaviour is that the two actors are exchanging information, and making sure that it is seen to be exchanged. The routine decision within the firm is to obtain fossets from Castor's. In exceptional circumstances, there is a secondary routine to follow. In a different environment, there might be a procedural manual – perhaps the TOMB *Quality Standard* – to which Jerry should refer. His instructions should be to obtain fossets from Pollux, and then report the change to his superior, or otherwise file details of his actions in an information system. If Castor's inability to supply starts to occur more than occasionally, it is perhaps time to review the routine procedure to approach them first. The information is feedback on the original decision to routinise the purchasing so that Jerry can proceed without having to seek permission every time there are fossets to be ordered.

In the formal environment of The Owner-Managed Business, there is probably neither a manual nor a written information system. The organisation will grow out of the BSQ phase when it establishes the MMM – or Monday Morning Meeting. This will be the perfect occasion for Jerry to observe that he has now had to approach Pollux four times in the last six weeks, or for Tom to ask how often Castor's have failed recently (as he saw Pollux fossets being used the other day), both parties leading up to the question of reviewing supplier priorities.

The MMM is not without its own difficulties. Its concept as an exchange of information amongst a smallish team of people who both know and need to know about events is laudable. Without feedback, there is no learning, and the meeting is therefore the source of learning. Unfortunately, because Tom owns the business, has worked there longer, knows every detail of what is happening (or wants to), is more interested anyway, and ultimately pays the others' wages, he will naturally dominate the meeting. If he is decisive, he will appear dogmatic; if discursive, he will appear uncertain. How he learns to cope with this is another story, but meanwhile, there is an information exchange taking place within the firm.

Responsibility and initiative

Further down the 'hierarchy', there is a lesser phenomenon to be observed, known as the *Rather Unnecessary Question.* Jerry may have an assistant, Minnie, who in undertaking work will tend naturally to ask Jerry what to do. Jerry, instinctively keen to devolve what responsibility there is, will reply to any question with, 'What do you think?' For example:

Minnie: Jerry, we are running out of 10mm fossets. What should I do?

Jerry (*without irony*): What do you think you should do?

Minnie: Er, I thought I might phone Castor's, or, if they are out of stock, get on to Pollux.

Jerry: That sounds fine to me, Minnie. Go ahead.

This is another demonstration of a learning process, where Minnie is demonstrating that she knows the procedure, informing Jerry of a situation, and also exploring the freedom of action available to her. Because she may not be doing this consciously, questions will continue to be raised as they occur until an occasional, but expected, review process is established. Meanwhile, Jerry can cure Minnie's unnecessary questioning of the rather obvious by appointing Spike as her assistant. Spike will now ask Minnie rather unnecessary questions which she will be able to answer.

Note that in the exchange above, Minnie observes, 'We are running out . . .' not 'We have run out . . .' This may be an important use of *initiative* (depending, of course, on the lead times for ordering fossets). In firms which are small enough for everyone to talk, the spoken word and initiative will be common; as the firm gets larger, there is a formalisation both of the instruction and the recording phase. Instead of someone spotting something and telling someone else about it, in a large organisation, a defined person is given the specific task of watching the fosset stock and noting when it reaches a certain level, and then recording their consequent actions. Every event has to be anticipated and then recorded. The recording is important because it has the potential to provide the feedback which may in due course cause procedures to be reviewed and revised. To the people required to do it, recording actions looks very much like a form of control; since it has no immediate impact on events, it must be a form of 'checking up'. This is particularly true if priorities change faster than procedures and certain record systems become irrelevant and unused. This is the dreaded slide towards the world where procedures become more important in their own right than people. Bureaucracies are created in which the nearest thing to a joke is the instruction: 'Yes, you may dispose of those files, but take a copy of them before you do.'

In the small firm, reporting the completion of instructions verbally may be seen as a form of attention-getting or approval-seeking, so people tend not to do it. In fact, someone else may be waiting to know something has been done (even though it was expected) before taking some contingent action. Closing the feedback loop is perplexingly difficult at times. This may be why entrepreneurs who build dynamic, rapidly-changing businesses tend to operate close to their staff, making sure that information comes straight to themselves personally, as well as going straight from them.

George Davis, who created the Next retailing chain out of a tired men's tailoring operation is popularly supposed to have required his store managers to phone him personally on Saturday evening with details of the week's takings (there being no Sunday trading in those days). With well over one hundred stores in the chain, this must have taken everyone involved quite a time. On a purely rational basis, it is hard to see what difference this could have made compared to the store managers faxing the figures to headquarters and someone consolidating them early on Monday morning. There are very few decisions that can be taken on a very short-term basis, and precise timing would not be critical in dealing with trends in performance. Perhaps, however, the point was one of involvement –getting to report your store's sales figures direct *to the man himself* was a sure reminder of who – and what – you worked for. It certainly seemed to be part of a successful formula; some say that George Davis's main fault was in growing Next so fast to begin with that he had to be sacrificed when the pace could not be sustained.

Information Technology

No discussion of information would be complete without a mention of *information technology* (IT). Indeed in the first draft, this chapter was to be left blank (save for an error message) in tribute to IT's persistent ability to defy the price-delivery-quality triangle (see Chapter 8) by supplying overdue projects which do not work properly, seriously over budget. Broadly, this is because organisations have historically been stuck with a system once they have bought it, and because when they bought it, they did not know what they were buying (or even what they bought it for). Consequently, they had to entrust it to some people who knew what it was (hardware and software engineers, systems analysts and programmers, applications consultants, and so on) – but these people did not know much about what their new employers wanted to achieve. This was like employing mechanics to be taxi drivers; the vehicles were well-maintained, but no one knew the best route to the chosen destination.[2]

Because knowledge of their employer's business was secondary to their own technical expertise, computer people spent much of their time seeking to deliver by computer the information system formerly operated by people. This is not necessarily what you would want to use, starting from scratch. For example, I am intrigued by the reference number on my telephone bill, which consists of 4 letters and 10 numerals. I know BT is a big company, but together, these provide for a potential 36 billion combinations. I happen to know that it is not my account number (I once had one of those when there were two different lines, and it was an 8-digit number) so what information does it contain? I am, for the most incontrovertible reasons, uniquely identifiable in the electronic database from my telephone number. The 14-character reference must be an anachronism.

For many years, the computer people called the tune about what you could and could not do with information (and perhaps they still do in places). 'Computer error' has been an excuse for some form of human failing – computers can only process the

---

[2] The current vogue is for people called architects, prefixed with words like systems, solutions, technical etc. A scan of newspaper advertising for IT consultants suggests that software experience is still regarded as more important than knowledge of clients' businesses.

data they are given – but 'computer failure' is still an acceptable norm. It is still common to phone organisations and be told that the operator cannot respond to your query because the system is down. Suppose you phoned and the telephone company said that the lines were not operating, or you went to the bank and they said that all the tills were locked. There has been modest uproar over the level of penalties for franchise railway companies failing to run sufficient trains, but it is still OK for 'the system to be down'.

In the interface between bureaucracy, where procedures dominate events, and computers, where events are reduced to records, strange things can happen. A Japanese friend of mine returned home once to find bailiffs sent by the electrical company hanging around in his front doorway trying to silence the burglar alarm. Mr Otsubo rented his house, and thanks to an initial error by the letting agent, he had originally notified the utility companies that he was responsible for supplies to number 21. Establishing that he in fact lived at number 21A, he notified the authorities again. The result was two electricity bills each quarter, one of which Mr Otsubo reconciled with his meter and paid; the other, he passed to the letting agent, who ignored it. It transpired that this second bill was his neighbour's from number 21. After the latter bills had remained unpaid for some time, bailiffs were sent to disconnect the meter. According to their information, the meter was now located inside Mr Otsubo's house. The computer said so. No one had moved the meter physically, but carelessly, almost criminally, someone had been allowed to move its location in the symbolic world within the computer. The person at number 21 had nothing to do with any of these events, though he did think it was 'a good laugh'. (For those of you who don't like loose ends, the bailiffs were perplexed by the alarm because they were not entitled to interfere with the electricity supply to it, as they usually are when they are sent to the correct house.)

The software used in an information system needs to be able to map the environment it represents. In the mathematical sense, a map is a unique relationship between two sets of things, which can take many forms. We are familiar with an Ordnance Survey map, which attempts to represent local topography to scale, except that it converts three dimensions into two, and uses symbols such as contour lines for the missing one. A road map maintains accurate distances along roads and preserves intersections, but it is vague about topography. The map of the London Underground preserves only sequences between, and line intersections at, stations; if you are travelling underground, the topography is irrelevant.[3] In setting out to build a computerised map which can be used to run a business, the first issue is to understand the topography of the firm, which is not a straightforward task. It may take 10 months to understand 90% of what is going on, but the remaining 10% can take 10 years to appreciate. Such depth of understanding is difficult to articulate, and much in demand. It is called *experience*.[4]

The second phase is to construct a set of mathematical relationships which correspond to the key dimensions of the firm's topography. Not everyone can do this, and it requires an aptitude which is not necessarily related to programming ability. Only once a rigorous model is built are the software skills needed, yet the rate of change in this field is sufficiently fast that major IT users feel they are obliged to employ young graduates with state-of-the-art knowledge. In Canada, there is a kind of systems 'finishing school' which graduates of all disciplines willingly pay to attend because the proprietors can actually guarantee jobs at the end, such is the demand from industry.

Where computing systems can be used to store reliable maps of the real world they can be exceedingly valuable, but where there is discrepancy, there is danger. One can argue that computers will not be able to produce perfect correspondence until such time as every possibility can be envisaged. Within a finite system, this is possible, and computers are now fast enough 'thinkers' to beat chess grand masters by exhaustive analysis of possible moves for example, but they will not recognise that Birnam Wood has come to Dunsinane, unless someone has forewarned them of the possibility. It is worth considering, along with all the acclaim for the role performed by IT systems in bringing back pictures from the Mars probe, that if

---

[3] In fact, the lack of topographic detail sometimes encourages visitors to London to take wasteful tube journeys such as Regent's Park to Great Portland Street, where the walk between platforms inside Baker Street Station, where you have to change trains, is further than the original journey by foot.

[4] It is an unfortunate complication that the intangible nature of experience enables lazy people to pass off inertia and conservatism as judgment.

the surface of the planet had been covered in say, milk chocolate, the system would not have recognised it unless some human being had first allowed for the possibility. If I transfer the text I have just written, prepared on a notebook computer, via floppy disk to my 'home' computer, I fancy the latter will tell me that the disk drive is not valid. This is not true, of course, because the 0.5mb diskette works fine in the laptop, it is just that the version of operating software on my home machine has not been told to expect 0.5mb floppies.

Looking ahead

Despite these and other criticisms that may fairly be levelled at the IT industry, information technology[5] is a different subject from Information itself. There have been remarkable advances in the way data is stored and transferred, and the speed at which iterative procedures can perform complex calculations makes possible many tasks which could not previously have been contemplated. The interesting question is how much use the world of business has made of these increased opportunities available to it. Aspects of information remain which essentially discourage its extensive use. Firstly, there is the 'paranoia' of secrecy; secondly, hierarchical organisations seem to equate status with rights to knowledge (and ignorance for juniors, therefore); finally, there is the paradox of information itself. Faced with a simple yes/no decision and no information, tossing a coin would yield a 50 per cent chance that you would choose the 'correct decision'; what would be the effect of collecting information bit by bit? You could form some differing conclusions about the use to which, for example, churches or outdoor marketplaces are put, if you observed for one day only. A week's worth of observations would be more useful, but how would you know it was sufficient – and would seven consecutive days be a more – or less – reliable guide than seven days selected at random from a longer period? Ultimately,

[5] The last word on IT goes to IT itself. I cannot imagine how I would have prepared this text without a word processing package – and as an appalling typist, I am dependent on the spell check for basic error correction. By and large, I am grateful for it, but somehow, when it turned up the phrase 'infuriating technology' it spoke volumes.

information in business is used in the context of making decisions, which are made by people who also operate in socio-political systems. Sometimes, too much information may not be helpful!

Advances in IT have undoubtedly made tasks achievable which not so long ago would have been thought impossible, and many consequent benefits have accrued in business processes and procedures. However, one is left with the feeling that for every achievement, there is probably another issue which IT has impeded, as one continues to hear stories of systems which do not allow invoices to be issued, or cannot cope with cash sales. This book is scheduled to appear shortly before digital television becomes available in the UK. This will be the point at which the parallel communication systems of computing and broadcasting do not so much converge as collide (to quote a spokesman for BT). The profound-sounding gTLD-MoU (Generic Top Level Domain Memorandum of Understanding), which allocates Internet designations, will come 'face-to-face' with people in their sitting rooms via the mundanely-named STB (set top box). What will the world of *Coronation Street* make of the Information Superhighway?

WHERE TO NEXT?

Information from the salesforce has limited value (Chapter 4)
The information surrounding the calculation of costs is important (Chapter 7)
Everyone needs to understand strategy (Chapter 11)
Because the effect is felt in the bottom line (Chapter 16)

20. Business accountability

People in business should work together to ***sell things repeatedly, over time, for more money than is spent in so doing****. There is no excuse if they do not*

If you are reading this book because you are interested in having a business of your own, it is to be hoped that you have found it valuable. Possibly, you may expect to be informed of how the general legislative framework, such as the system of taxation and the Companies Acts, affects business. In that case, you will be disappointed, but perhaps you will succeed in generating the necessary income to pay professional advisors to advise you. The first thing lawyers will tell you is that legal advice is worth what you pay for it. A derivative of this might be that the more money you have, the more you can afford to use the law on your side.

In the days of the 'enterprise culture' when we ran our enterprise training company, we would sometimes meet with other course providers with whom we were at the same time professional colleagues and business rivals. On one occasion someone examined our course outline and remarked, 'Where's the bookkeeping?', to which my partner replied – impressively, I thought – that if we are teaching people to play cricket we don't begin with the intricacies of the scoring system. The analogy is sound; at cricket, people need to be able to bat, bowl and field first, then they can develop some notion of scoring. Only when they are engaged in serious competition does the equitable and foolproof – but also arcane – score-keeping system make an entry. In business, you need customers and the capabilities to supply them first. Some notion of profit or cash flow is required also, but there is no need to bother with recording systems until there is something to record. On this occasion, the other person was ahead of us. 'Yes,' he replied, 'I know – but people *expect* bookkeeping on courses like this.'

This is true. We ran a wide range and large number of courses for aspiring entrepreneurs, under contract to the Department of Employment, at the time a separate entity from Education. Their popularity eventually declined – not with the public, but through pressure on the government to provide training for the increasing number of unemployed people in the recession of the 1990s. Government funding passed through different channels, and the initiative was lost; sadly no one was able or prepared to compare the benefits – and hence the justifiable costs – of assisting someone not just to fill a job vacancy, but to create their own employment. Even when there were selection interviews, these courses were intended to provide the most open access available, with the only criterion being people's genuine interest in and desire to start a business. Individuals came from all backgrounds; there were refugees from Vietnam and people from other minorities, including by coincidence, three PhDs in one group of sixteen.

When we asked people why they wanted to join a course, most of them would cite learning about 'the business side' as a reason. Asked to elaborate, people would name tax, law, bookkeeping . . . and run out of topics, still leaving the feeling that there was something else, too inaccessible even to name, but something that a course would address.

This last belief would usually turn out to be true, but not in the way most people expected. The real benefits of the course were that they helped people to articulate, clarify and evaluate their ideas *from a business perspective*, the need for which was not something generally appreciated in advance. When we tried to explain this, it tended to put people off, so we allowed the idea of 'the business side' to persist, unharmed.

There were courses provided by other organisations where bookkeeping featured prominently, but we refused to believe that it was a useful tool in business planning. In our courses it did not feature until people had first written a business plan. In one cooperative venture, our fellow trainers scheduled bookkeeping for the first morning of a special course for the visually impaired (who would have a good reason for not using conventional bookkeeping anyway), because that was the time that suited the lecturer best! We were both surprised and disappointed at what we regarded as a second rate decision – but moving from the education system to the 'real world' (we had stepped out of teaching roles in a postgraduate business school) is always a shock. Higher education aspires to perfection, whereas in work, ordinariness will usually do, much to the surprise of graduate recruits. The reason that many things at work are done the way they are is given by the people who do them as 'because that is how we do them'. This usually means that it achieves the desired result, but it does not imply that the method is at all best practice.

Probably, the design of courses mattered less than we thought, but in the early days, it was our business, and we – as typical new business owners – wanted to give the best. People's own enthusiasm counted more than anything and carried them through when they were suitably motivated. The 'business side' topics became less important as they were revealed. Awareness of the tax system may be necessary, but it only matters if there are profits to be taxed.[1] Knowing something of the legal framework in which business operates may tell you what you cannot do, but it does not tell you what you should do. Devising a bookkeeping system is definitely best done when there are some entries to make. Having a beautiful set of books and no customers leaves – well – plenty of time to colour them in.

The concept of the 'inaccessible something' of business pervades, effectively, as part of our mainstream culture. (There are certain ethnic minorities in Britain for whom business holds no mystery.) MBA students who may have worked in industry and commerce for some years still begin their courses with strange expectations. They are not surprised by *accounting*, but some regard *marketing* as a minority, almost irrelevant subject, instead of something without which business is difficult to contemplate. Broadly, this expectation can only change if the business world and its norms – which account for the majority of employment and nearly all discretionary family expenditure – are included within the common curriculum, but it is difficult to see how this will ever happen when teachers go straight from learning to teaching. (The use of business-type projects in schools is promising, though.) The alternative is for business to feature in the media – notably on television – but without excessive dramatisation, it makes rather dull subject matter, and again, it is not a topic people who work in television tend to know much about. There have been attempts to make business training more interesting, such as through the videos featuring

[1] Actually, the VAT registration decision can be quite important.

John Cleese, but the impression one forms as a teacher is that the funnier the presentation, the more the proper content is obscured.

Accountability and accounting

If you have read the other chapters, you will recognise that in business you do need a system of accounting. By analogy, you do need to count the runs at cricket, otherwise it is pretty pointless. (Some people would claim it is pointless anyway, of course.) You need to know the financial consequences of your decisions whenever possible *before* you take them. Bookkeeping does not help with this – it merely records transactions after they have occurred. The double-entry system which, as explained in Chapter 13 occurs naturally, records transactions in a close-to-foolproof way, but in your own business, you may choose any system you like provided it is consistent, and it runs on common sense. There are any number of pre-printed books and software packages available for sale, yet the majority have only two columns – for entering the mysterious credits and debits. In keeping most important accounts, a sensible person would want to record the balance as well as the individual entries, in order to know for example how much is owed by and to the business. The most important of all is to have a continuous record of the bank balance. This is a discipline we know from everyday life, yet many pre-printed versions of the accountancy profession's simplified bookkeeping system – something called the analysed cash book, which records payments and receipts under various categories – do not include a column for the bank balance.

Banks lend small businesses money on the basis of cash flow forecasts, which is sensible. They then expect owner-managers to control their businesses by comparing actual cash flows with the forecasts, which is not. There can be two very distinct reasons for not having a cash outflow – because you haven't incurred a liability, or because you haven't settled it. The important moment is when you take the decision which incurs the liability in the first place. At some point in the future, you will need cash to settle it.

Of course, if everything is running smoothly with the business profitable and a healthy positive cash flow (remember that you can have one of these without the other) the need to calculate future liabilities of a routine nature is much reduced, which is the case with the majority of business activity. In these circumstances, there are excellent opportunities for the subject of bookkeeping to take centre stage – along with its principal exponent, the accountancy profession.

The people in search of 'the business side' are generally of the opinion that 'accountants know', but accountants have been known to advise companies depending on telephone sales of advertising to aim to reduce their phone bills, to advise independent jewellers not to take on extra work because they will have to register for VAT, and to advise against claiming the legitimate use of part of the home for fear that it might one day give rise to capital gains tax. Accountants can devise costing systems which have all the staff huddled in one corner of a building, and they appear to have devised a method (though this is speculation) by which the closure of one more British coal mine transfers a further burden on to the remainder, and causes the next one on the list to be 'uneconomic'. The bodies to which accountants belong insist upon their members undergoing some form of continuous professional development, but they still belong to the world of work, where adequacy and not excellence are the norm.

Still, it would be ill-advised to make sweeping observations about the profession. The largest firms all have extensive management consultancy operations (sometimes confusingly bearing the same name as the accountants) which undertake all manner of assignments in fields ranging from software development to executive selection. The basic relationship with a client is however through the audit, a legal requirement imposed upon corporations requiring the appointment of a professionally recognised independent firm. There have in recent years been many questions asked about the relationship between client and auditor, in particular concerning which party's best interests are served by it. Seven years after the event for example, an enormous legal action hangs over the auditors of the Bank of Credit and Commerce International who seemed to think its affairs were in order a few months before it was closed down by the Bank of England and subsequently put into liquidation.

Ownership and control

The origins of auditing lie in the separation of the ownership from the management – and thence the control – of businesses. As capital markets developed, so wealthy individuals and savings institutions needed to know that the actions of people managing their businesses would not give rise to further financial commitments on their behalf, and in the nineteenth century this need was eventually enshrined in legislation in the form of limited liability. This appears on first acquaintance a strange concept, and it was satirised at the time by W S Gilbert in *The Gondoliers* through the character of the Duke of Plaza-Toro. In Act 1, he enters essentially destitute, only to reappear in Act 2 as the rich and powerful Duke of Plaza-Toro Limited. Limited liability means literally that the liability of the investors (properly called the members of the company) is limited to the amount they agree to subscribe. Whatever happens in the course of trade, they will not be required to meet any further debts, unlike say, syndicate members at Lloyd's of London (who have experienced some trouble in recent years). This provision makes considerable sense from a viewpoint of encouraging investment, but of course it means that the ability of the company to meet its debts is also limited. For the unscrupulous, this presented an opportunity to make money at other people's expense rather than through fair trade, an issue which was not directly addressed by Parliament until the Insolvency Act of 1985, which rendered people personally liable who knowingly or deliberately exploited the limited liability of their companies to the detriment of creditors.

The need to provide protection against fraud by the managers of limited companies, both for their investors and their trading partners, is reflected in the requirement of the audit, resulting in published accounts which are circulated to members and filed for public inspection at Companies House. There has been much wrangling over what information should be disclosed in these accounts, since it has generally been management's view that everything is commercially confidential. Indeed, it is only since 1967 that UK companies have been required to publish the value of their sales – something they tended to do reluctantly, using the euphemism 'turnover'. Nowadays, companies are of course proud of their sales figures, though 'earnings' is still preferred to the word 'profit'.

Whatever is actually disclosed, the accounts include a statement from the auditors which is carefully worded according to the latest legislation, but should essentially mean that the auditors have examined the books of the company in detail, and concluded that the management have conducted their affairs in a straightforward manner. This requirement gave rise to another irony, for in the case of companies which were actually managed by their owners – the vast majority of small companies, though not of small business, most of which do not have limited liability – they were required to pay accountants for the assurance that they were not defrauding themselves. The audit's more obvious purpose in this case was to prepare accounts for the Inland Revenue. The requirement for an audit for very small firms was removed by the European Union in 1994, and it remains to be seen how this will affect the activities of small accountancy practices.

Auditing is a retrospective activity, which involves looking backwards through records, checking for accuracy, noting anomalies, and categorising expenditure. It may be true that accountants no longer count their clients' postage stamps as they once used to, but they are still primarily concerned with whether something which took place a while ago was in any sense material to the present. Remote ownership, which is thus 'protected', still gives rise to shareholders being presented with results rather than future plans, and while shareholders have rights – which large institutional shareholders such as pension funds and insurance companies are sometimes criticised for not exercising – they are only to vote people to and from the board of directors. Just about the only time shareholders can vote for a plan is in takeover bids and mergers, where promises sometimes seem to be broken in the carefree manner of holiday romances.

Organisation and empowerment

Company directors are responsible to shareholders for the actions of the company's employees, and so there is accountability throughout an organisation. In terms of hierarchical management, the issue is whether focus should be on what has happened (management accounting) or what will happen (strategic planning). The liberated, learning organisation should be able to convert an individual manager's responsibilities under an agreed corporate strategy into an action plan and budget. Indeed, in the manner of an owner-manager, perhaps assisted with a course in business planning, managers in organisations should be able to do this for themselves, exploring the range of degrees of freedom to make decisions and the extent to which matters are at their personal discretion. Some senior people feel this will show their subordinates just how controlled and restricted they are, but experience says that people are better for knowing – they appreciate understanding their responsibilities and limits. This is called empowerment, one of the buzzwords of the late twentieth century.

Under the empowerment system, 'blanket approval' is given for normal actions. Unanticipated events only are referred to a superior, who should be as interested in, and concerned about, results which are better than expected as with under-performance. Being unable to cope with demand is, from a strategic perspective, just as bad a performance as being under target. This way, the manager gets on with doing 'it' while the superior is left to query whether 'it' is the right thing to be doing. Of course, the system assumes everybody is competent.

Paranoid – or possibly constipated – hierarchies tend to want 'controlled empowerment', where managers are free to do whatever they choose – provided they check with their superiors first. This is 'empowerment without the power' and a nonsense. This type of hierarchy insists on knowing what its subordinates did yesterday before agreeing their plan for today. Bosses then complain about their managers being unwilling to use initiative. Mostly, they waste each other's time while work continues much the same as it ever did.

Time management

According to Einsteinian physics, the point at which you read this is an event. This is not to imply that the fact you are actually reading is particularly remarkable, nor that the words will have a dramatic effect on your life. It is merely that 'event' is the term given to a point in the four-dimensional space-time continuum of Einsteinian physics. According to the theories, it may be possible – using machines as yet unavailable – to move around the continuum in all four dimensions instead of the three we are used to. Until that time comes – sorry, until that event occurs – it is not possible. Einstein may have said there is no such thing as *the* time, but provided we adjust our watches on aeroplanes, there undoubtedly is.

You cannot ask time to do something for you when you are unavailable, or get it to run slower if you are behind with your work. It does not go on holiday, and it will not wait while you finish your lunch, nor produce a report on what it has been up to. Even the arrival of the Chairman cannot deflect time from its course. I cannot, Einstein could not, and you cannot *manage time*.

The expression 'time management' must therefore mean something else, and it is one of those issues which occurs in the human interface within the workplace. The point of raising it usually seems to be when it needs improving, rather than when it draws praise, in the appraisal process for example. It is not the same thing as timekeeping (delivering the person at an appointed time) so much as deadline-meeting (delivering things), but it is more subtle than that. It seems to distinguish between the achievement of tasks in a straightforward, unruffled manner, and chaotic, last-minute crisis aversion. People can be said to do good work, but need to improve their time management, which raises questions about what constitutes *being at work* and what constitutes *getting on with one's work*.

I must admit that shortly after I embarked upon my career in business education and development, I was introduced to someone who asked me to submit a proposal for a short course on time management. I never got round to doing it. In truth, I did not really feel qualified, as I could not see a link between personal organisation at work and my speciality, which was strategic thinking. Looking back, it is hard to say when the realisation came about, but of course the two are closely connected. In business everything interconnects. There are issues of *self*-management – actually doing something rather than nothing, and completing things once they are started – but allocating time to and ordering the sequence of activities is all about priority setting. This does not mean doing everything that is urgent, and leaving everything else until it becomes so. Setting priorities comes from knowing what is important to the organisation that employs you – what it is trying to achieve commercially – and how what you do interrelates with the activities of the people around you. It comes, in short, from *understanding business.*

WHERE TO NEXT?

Control begins with marketing campaigns (Chapter 3)
Costs need understanding as well as controlling (Chapter 7)
Strategy translates into concerted action (Chapter 11)
Whatever it is, there is no point if it's not for profit (Chapter 16)
Alternatively: this is The End!

Index